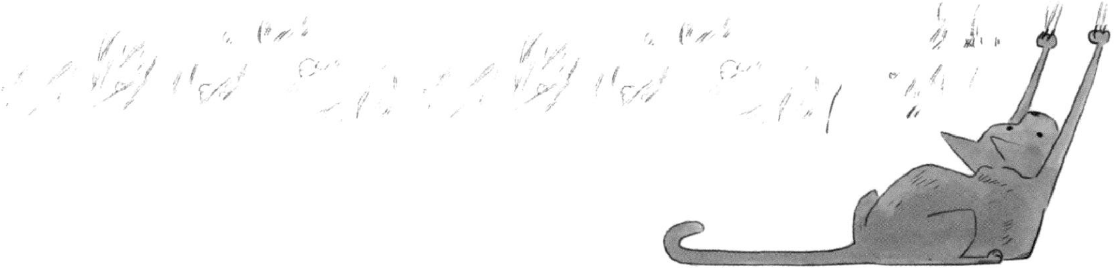

JONESY

JONESY

ISBN: 9781785659263

Published by
Titan Books
A division of Titan Publishing Group Ltd
144 Southwark Street
London
SE1 0UP

www.titanbooks.com

First edition: October 2018

10 9 8 7 6 5 4 3 2 1

All illustrations created and supplied by Rory Lucey.

Did you enjoy this book? We love to hear from our readers. Please e-mail us at: readerfeedback@titanemail.com or write to Reader Feedback at the above address.

To receive advance information, news, competitions, and exclusive offers online, please sign up for the Titan newsletter on our website: www.titanbooks.com

A CIP catalogue record for this title is available from the British Library.

Printed in Europe

JONESY

NINE LIVES ON THE NOSTROMO

RORY LUCEY

TITAN BOOKS

DEDICATION

For Emily and Caesar, my Ripley and Jonesy.

INTRODUCTION

A few years ago, after convincing my wife to watch *Alien* with me, she only wanted to know one thing before we began: "Does the cat die?" For a movie that ends with two survivors, we really don't get to see much of what the cat, Jonesy, is up to throughout the film. I viewed *Alien* that night wondering what life might be like for a non-human/non-xenomorph creature aboard the *Nostromo*. As a person who lives with a feisty orange feline, this is what I imagined nine lives on the *Nostromo* might be like...

– RORY LUCEY

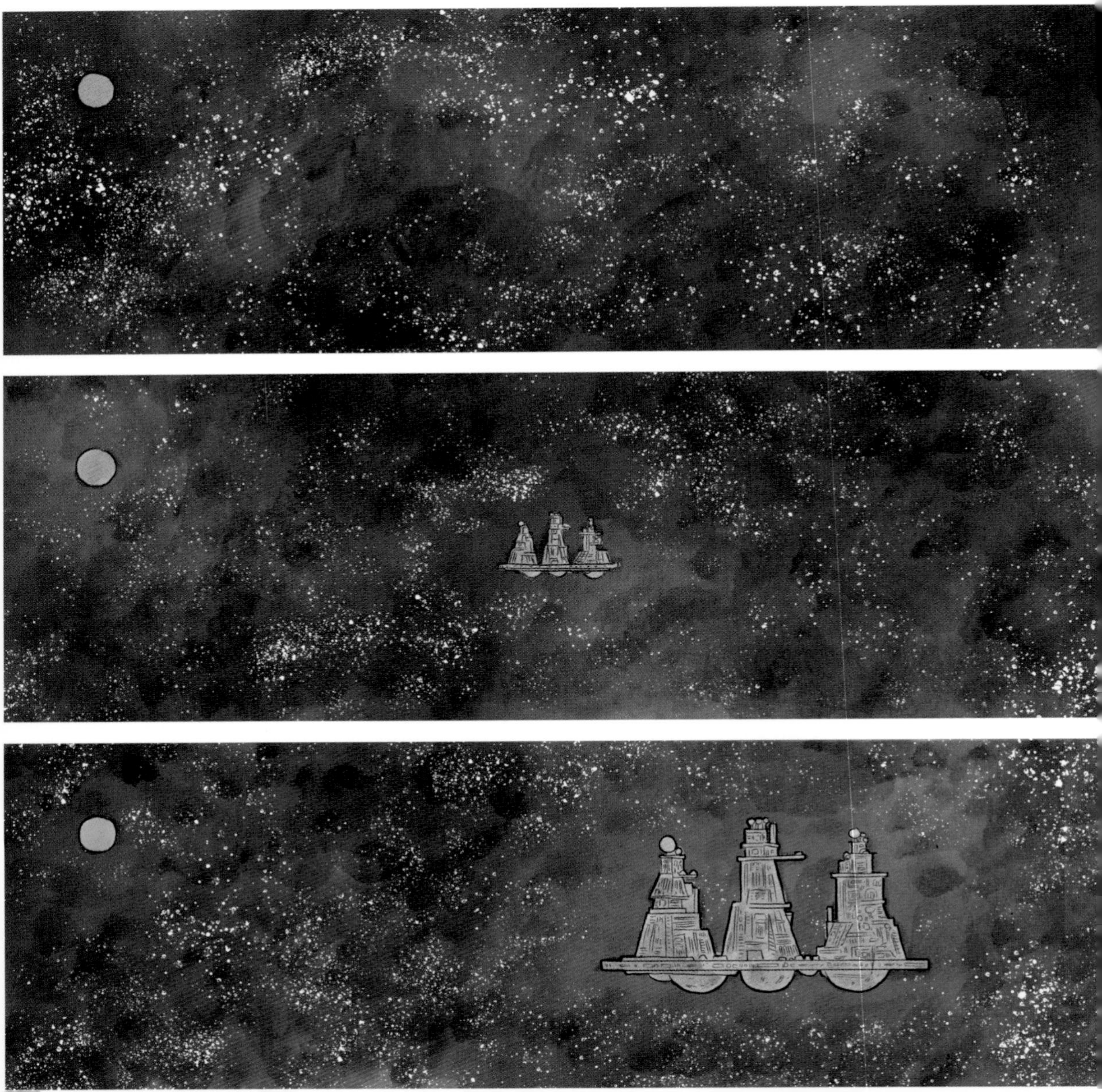

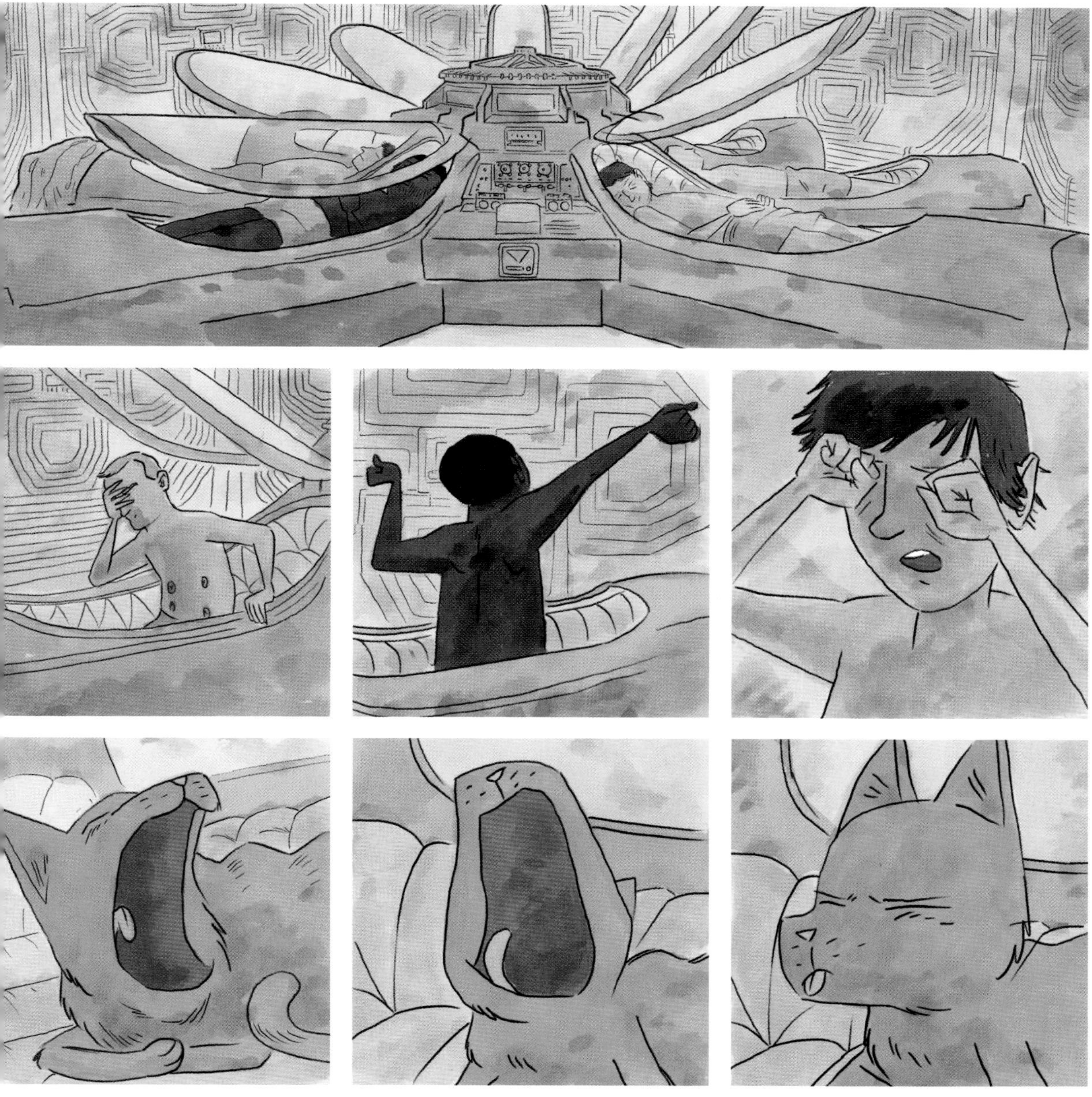

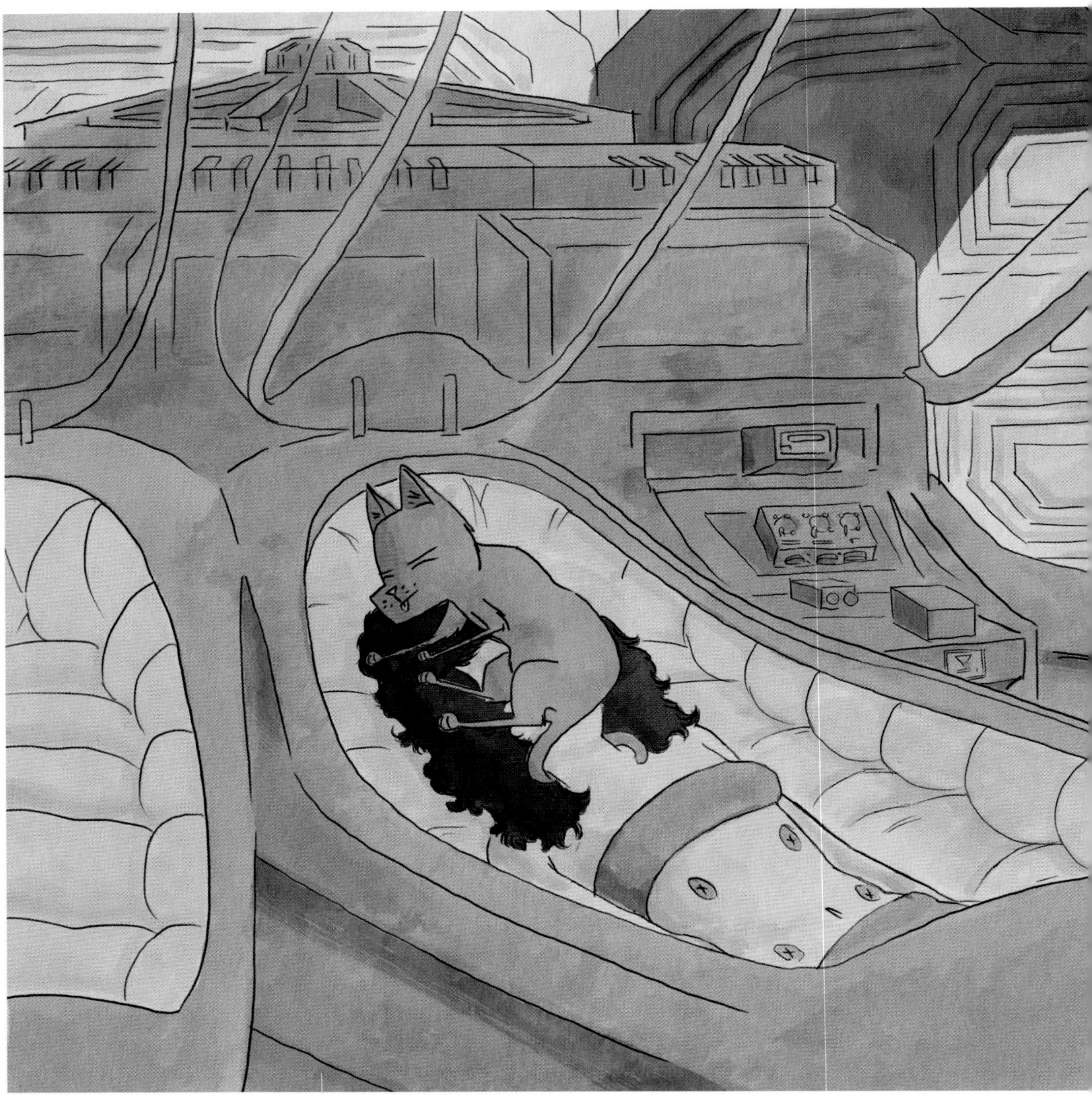

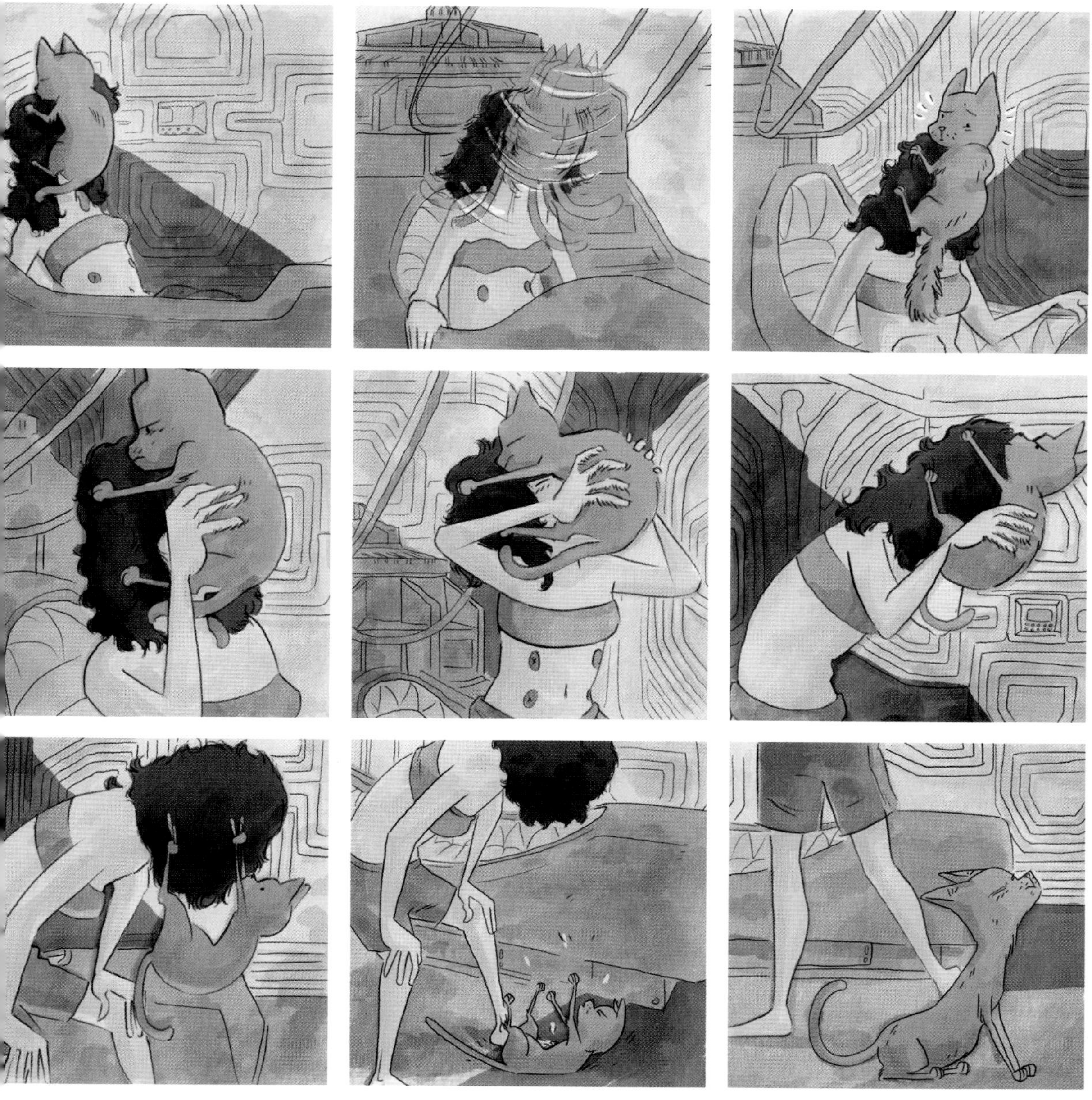

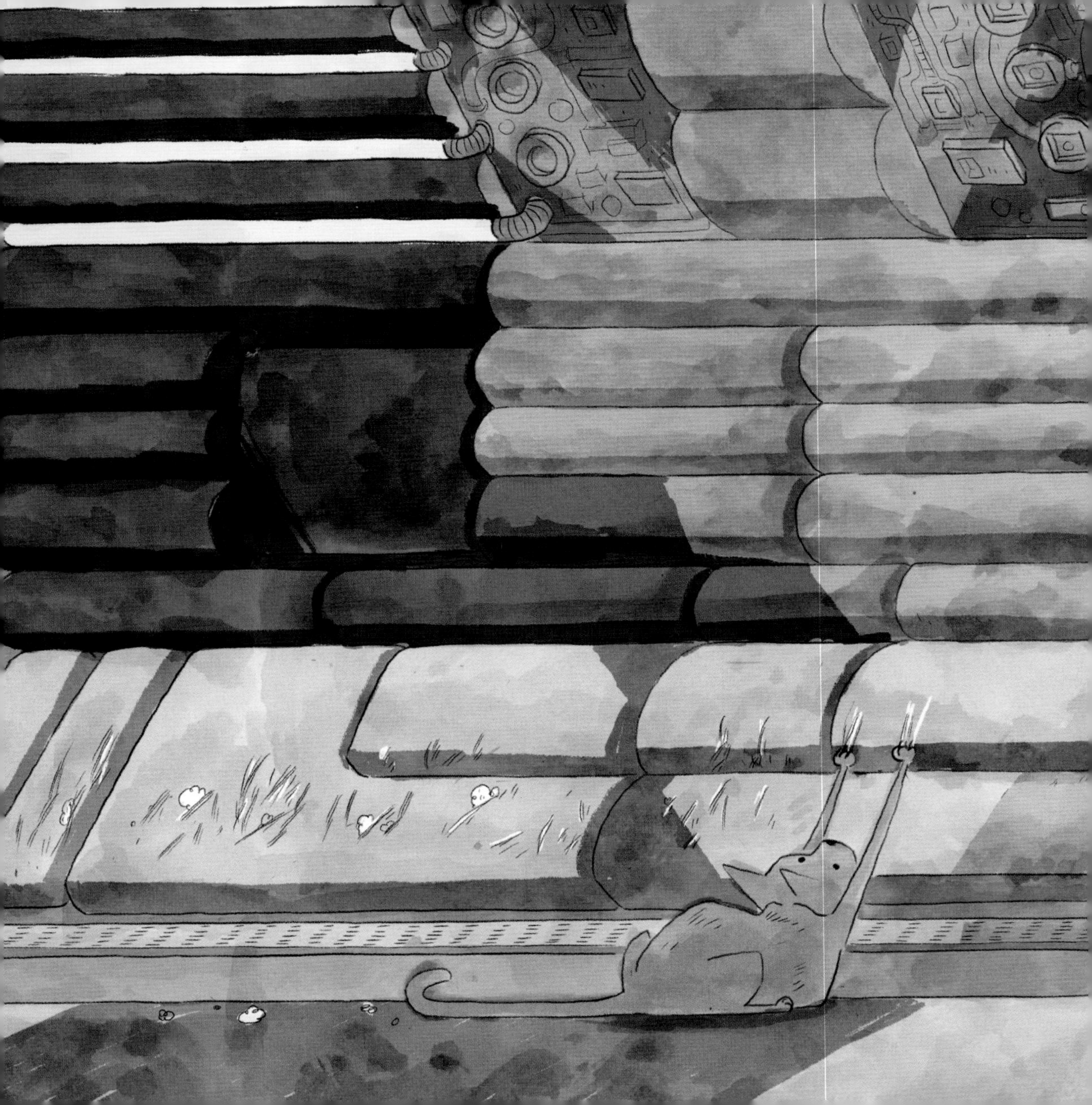

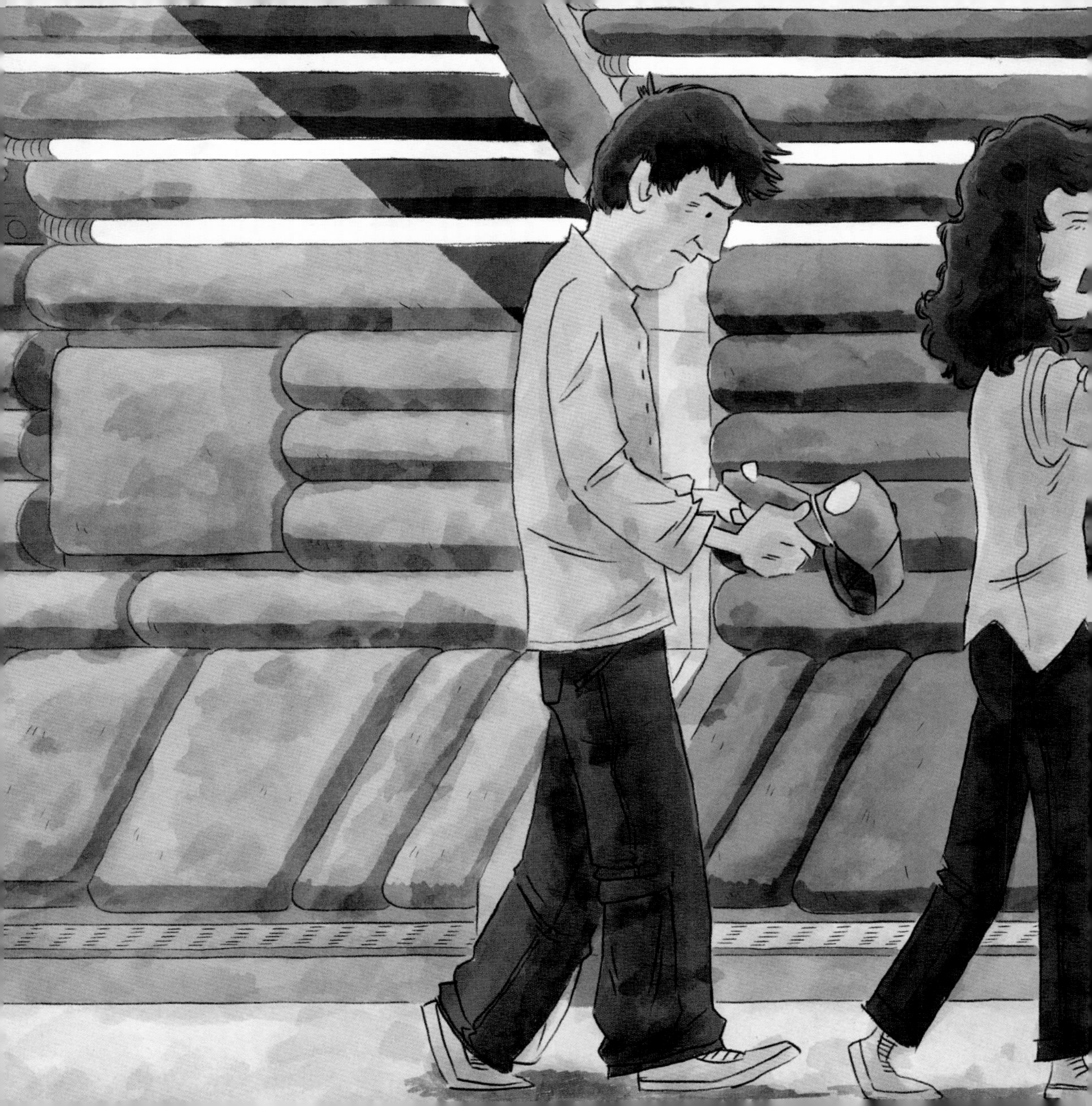

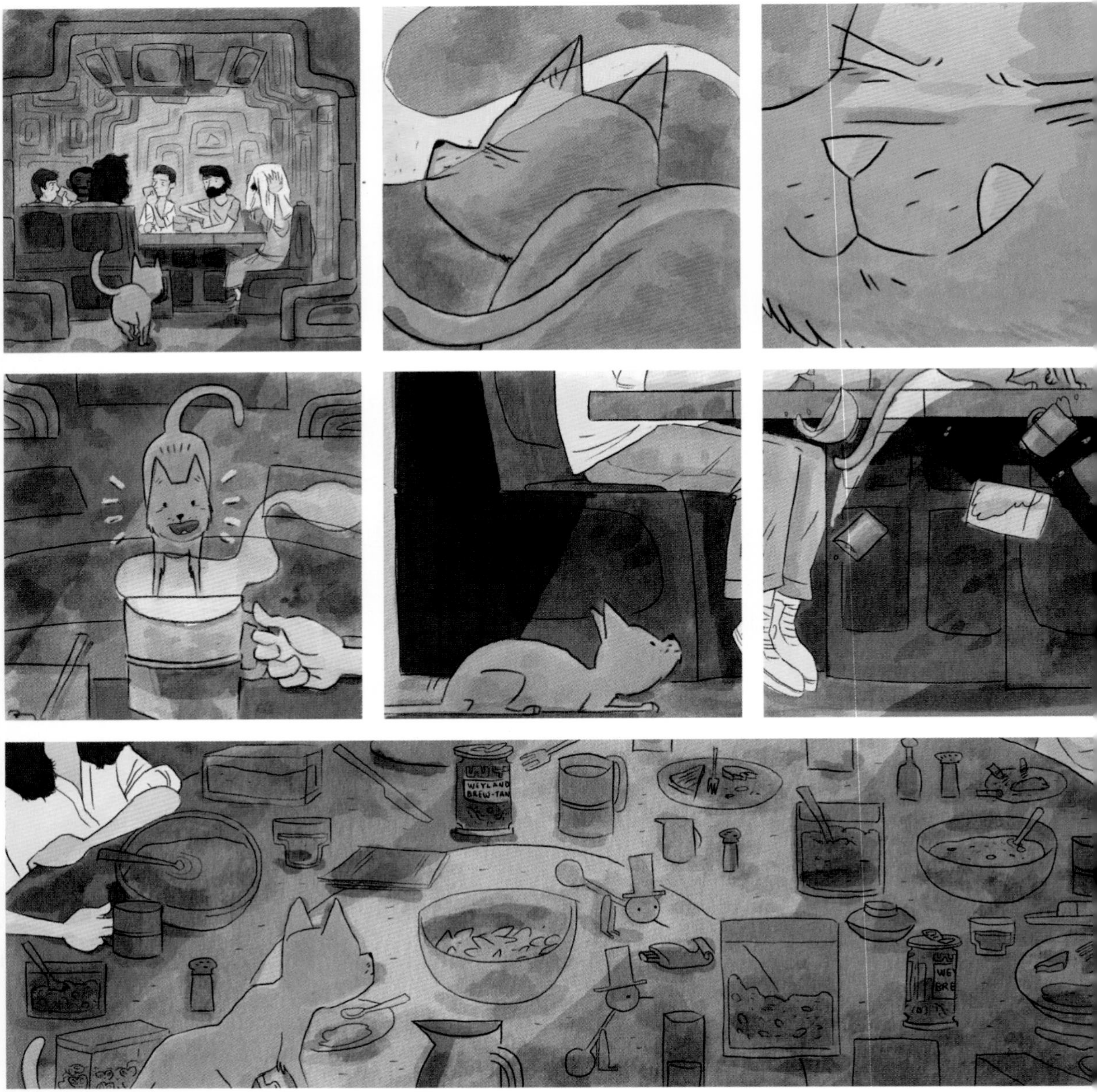
WEYLAND
BREW-TAN

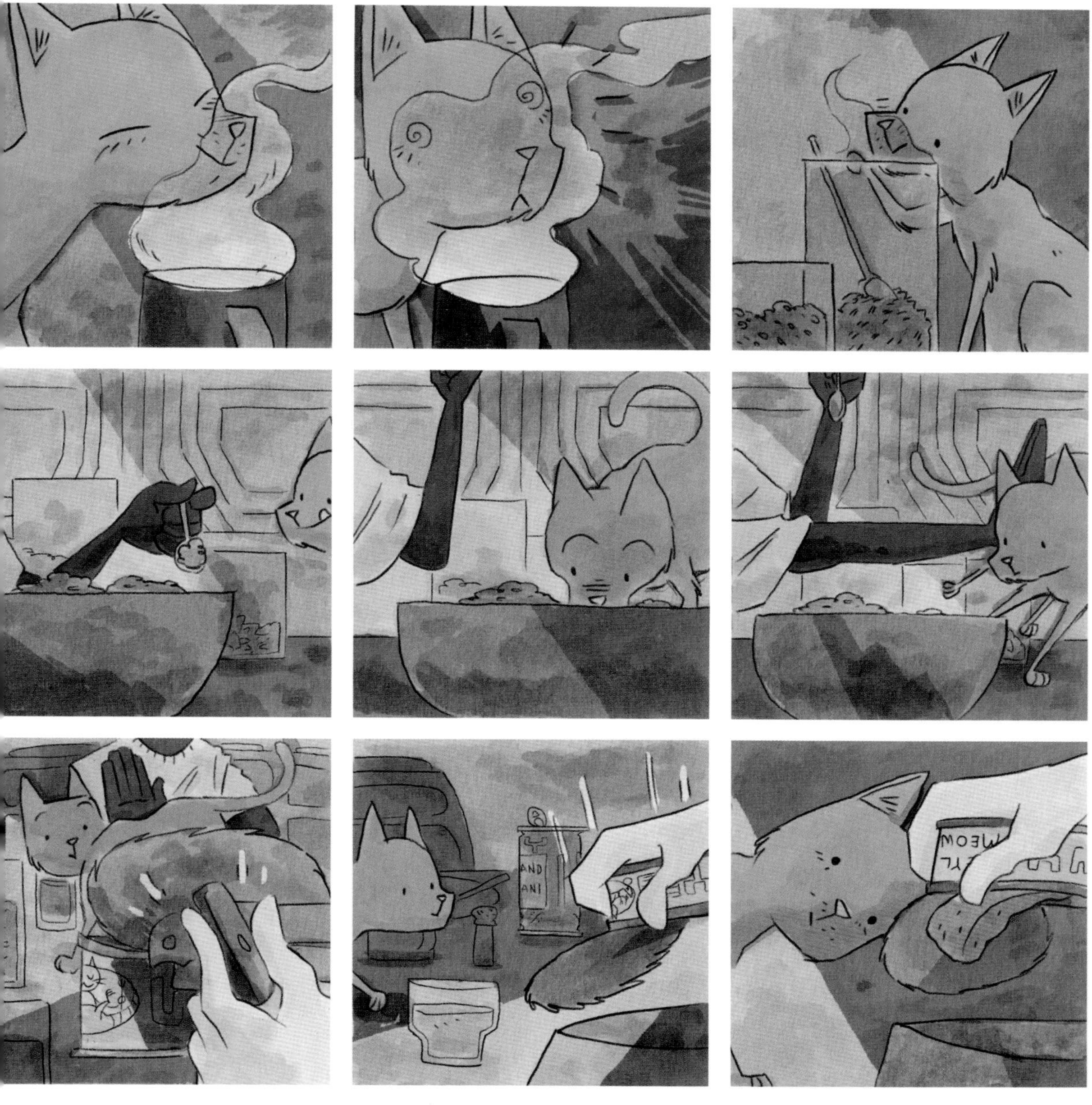
AND
ANI

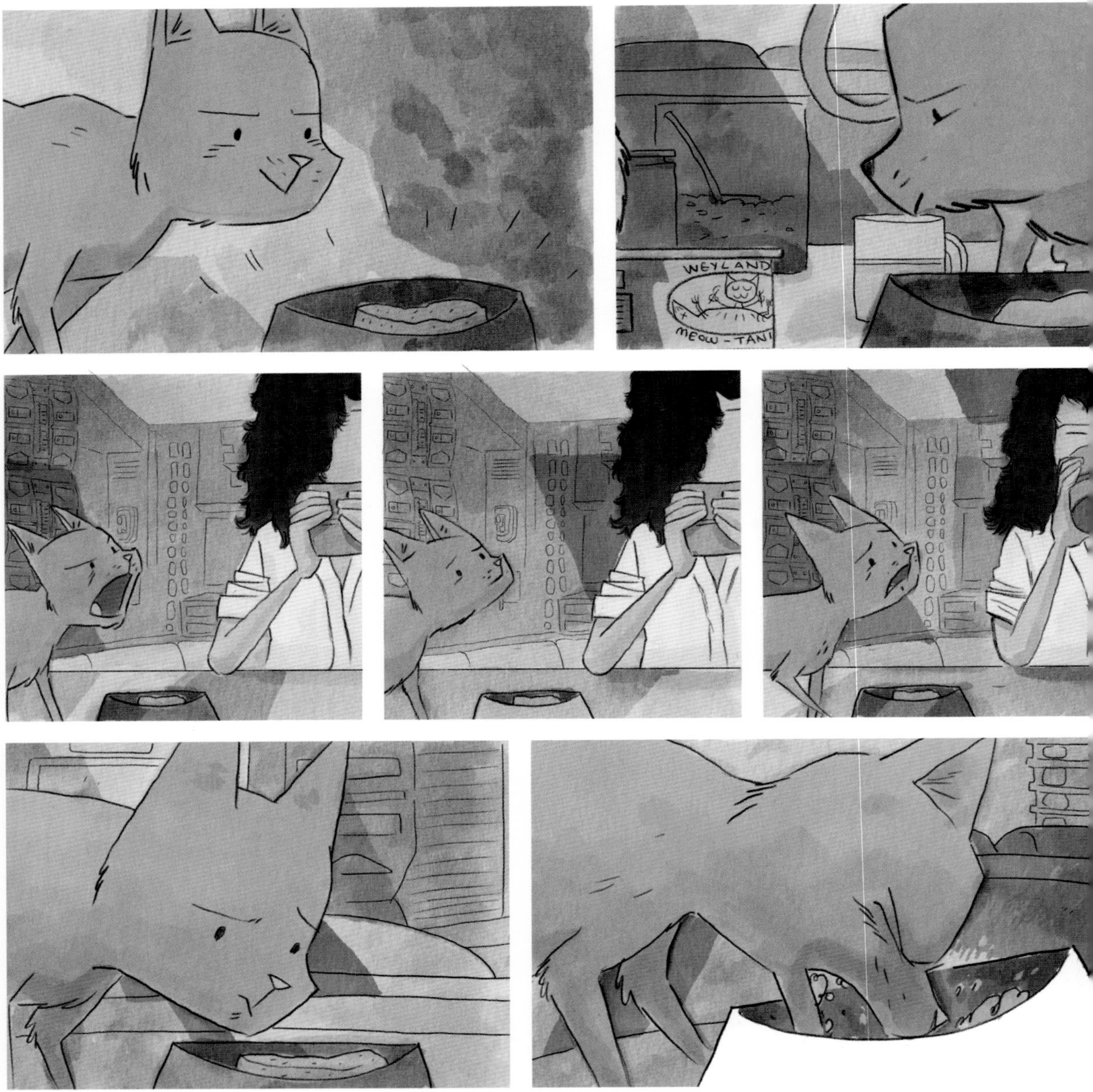
WEYLAND
MEOW - TAN

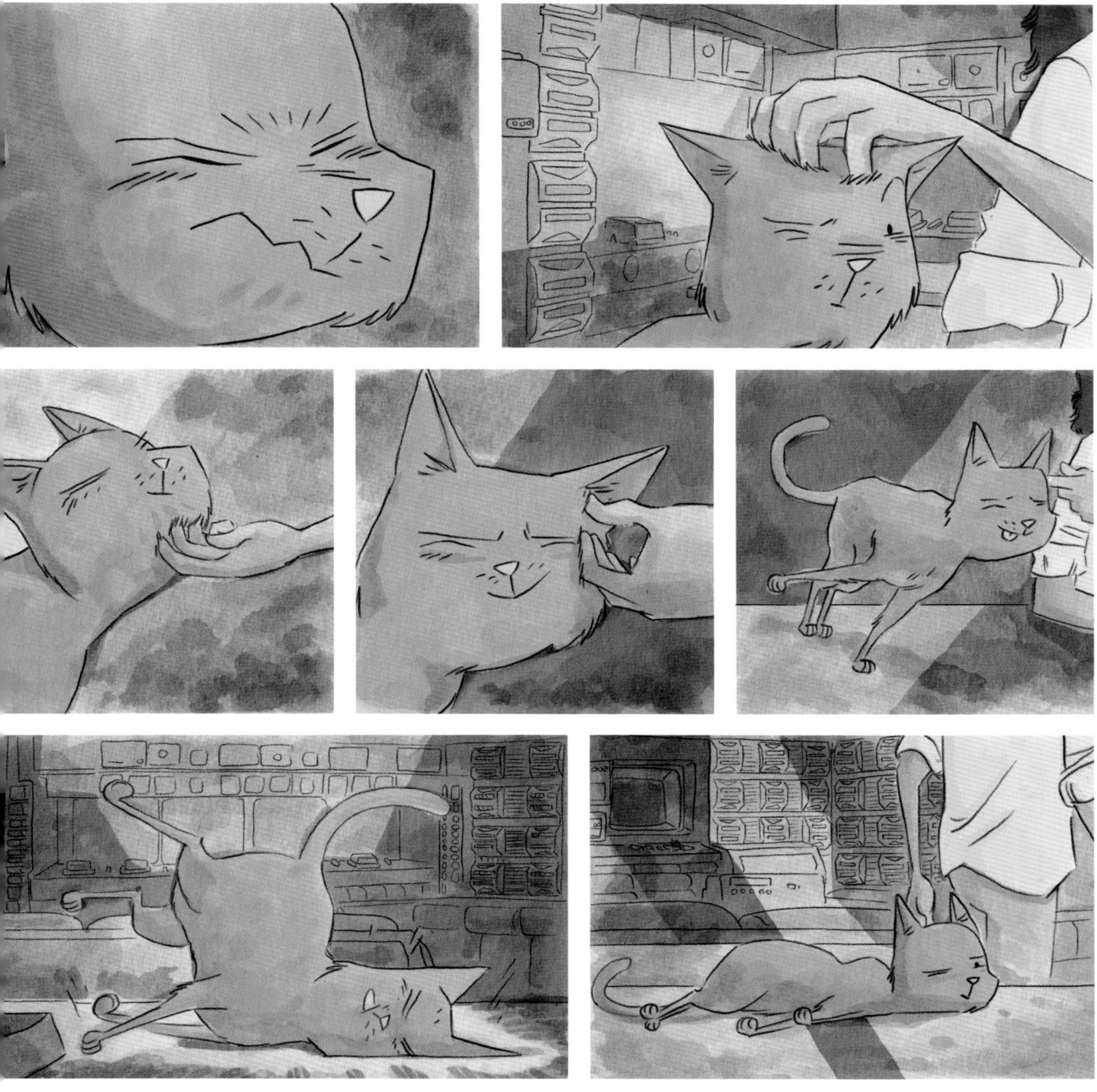

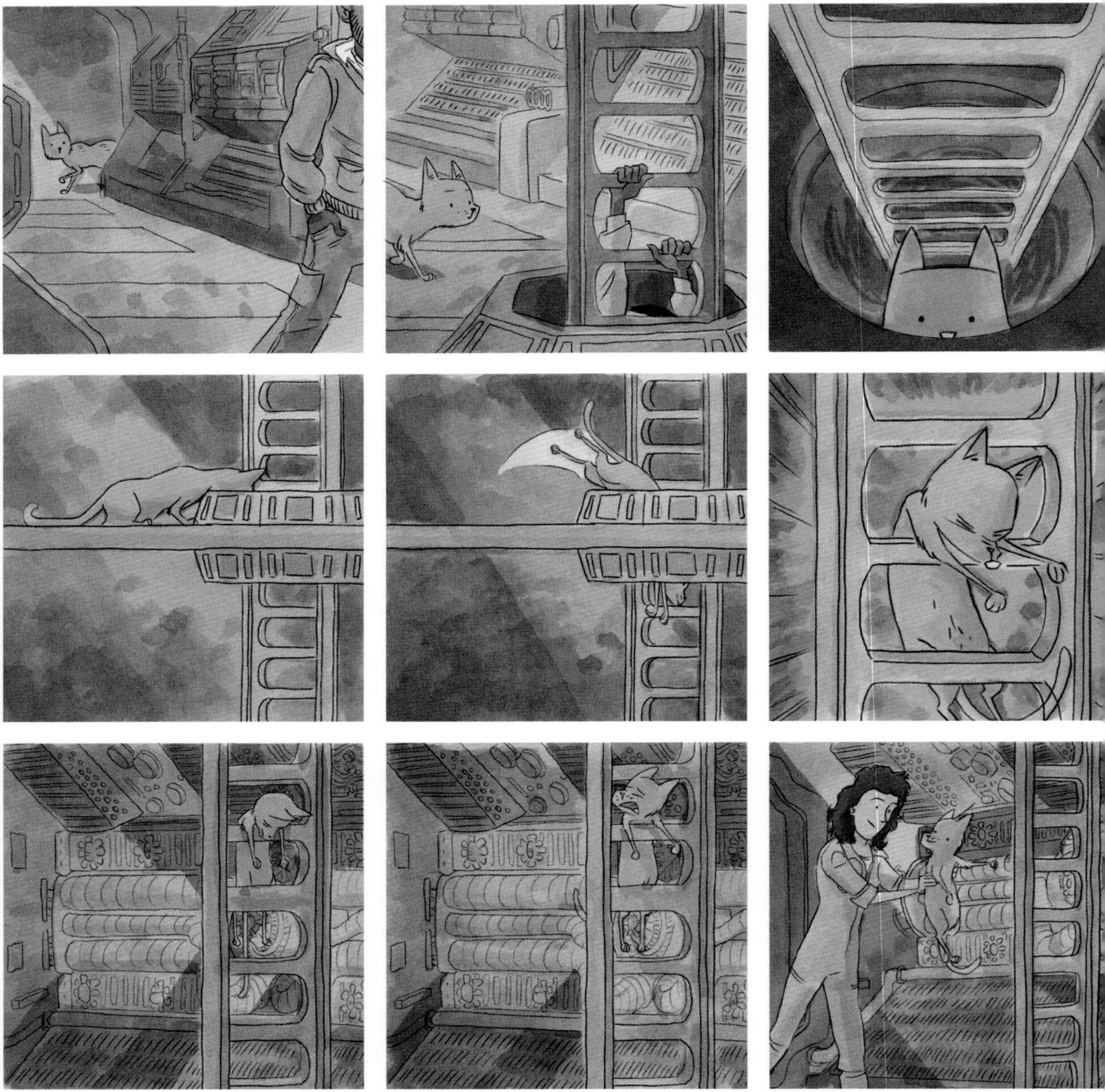

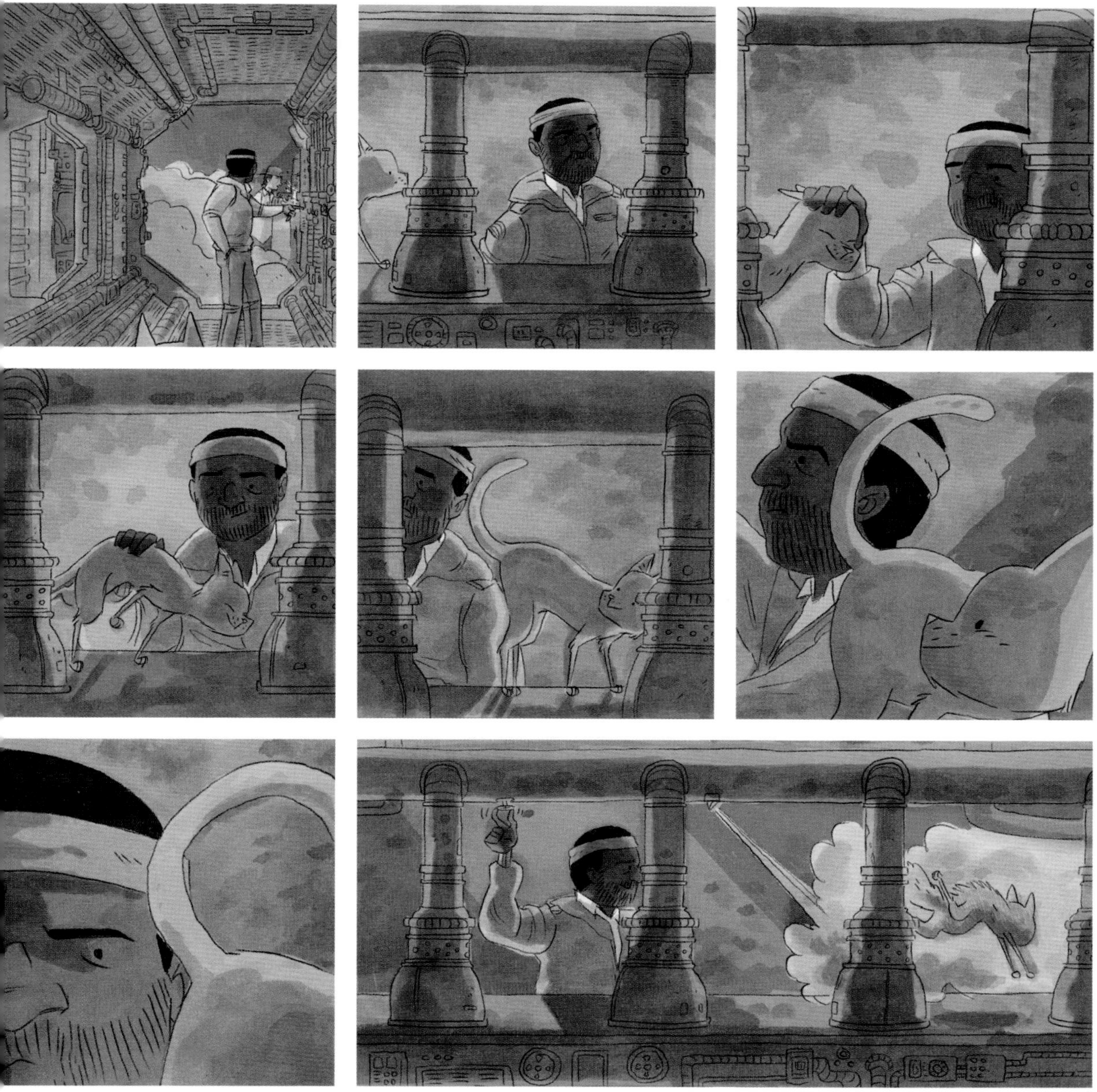

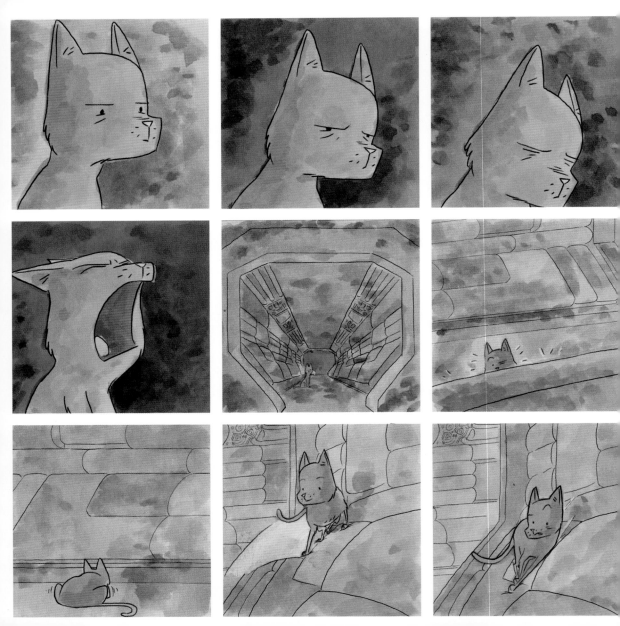

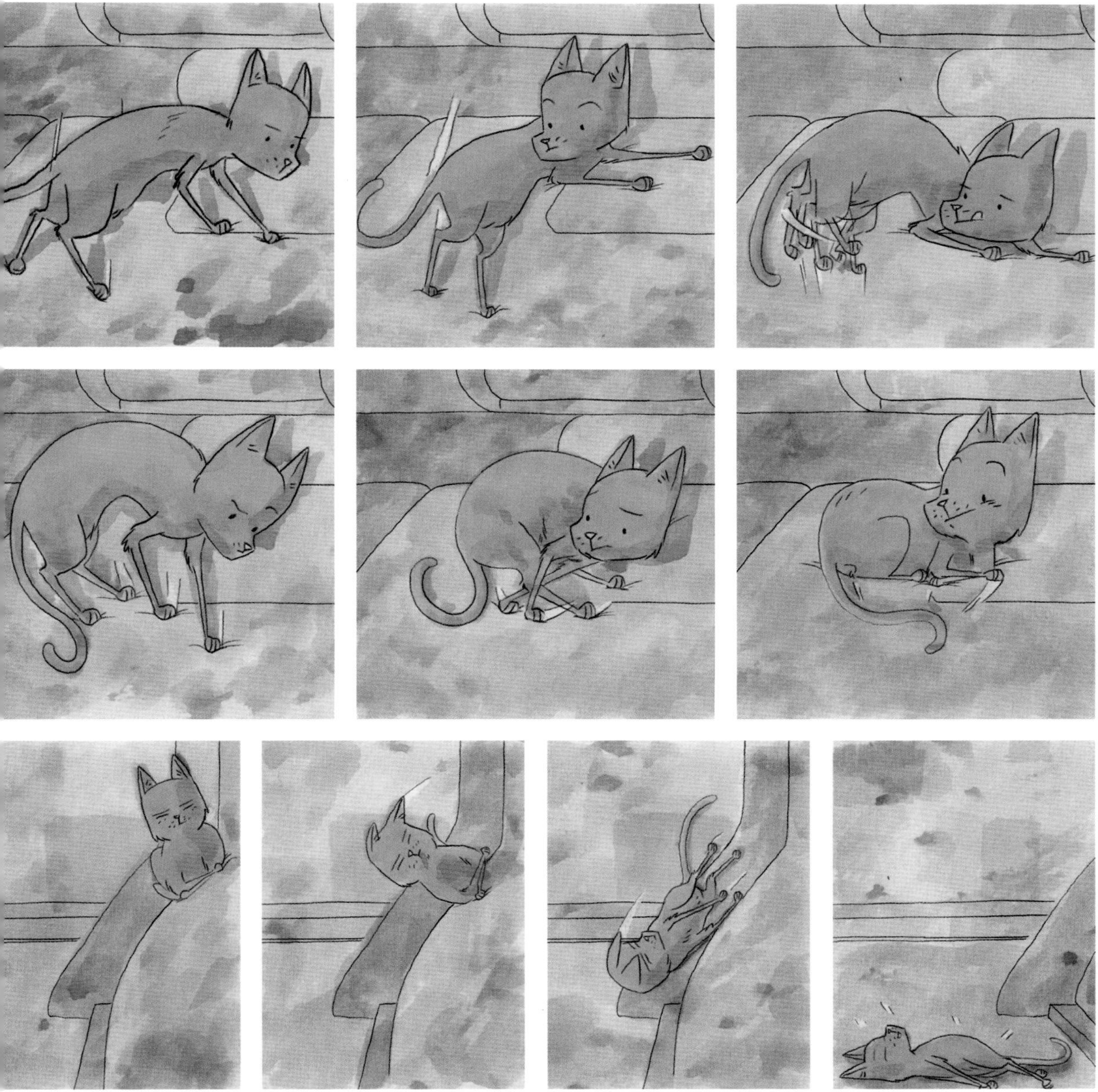

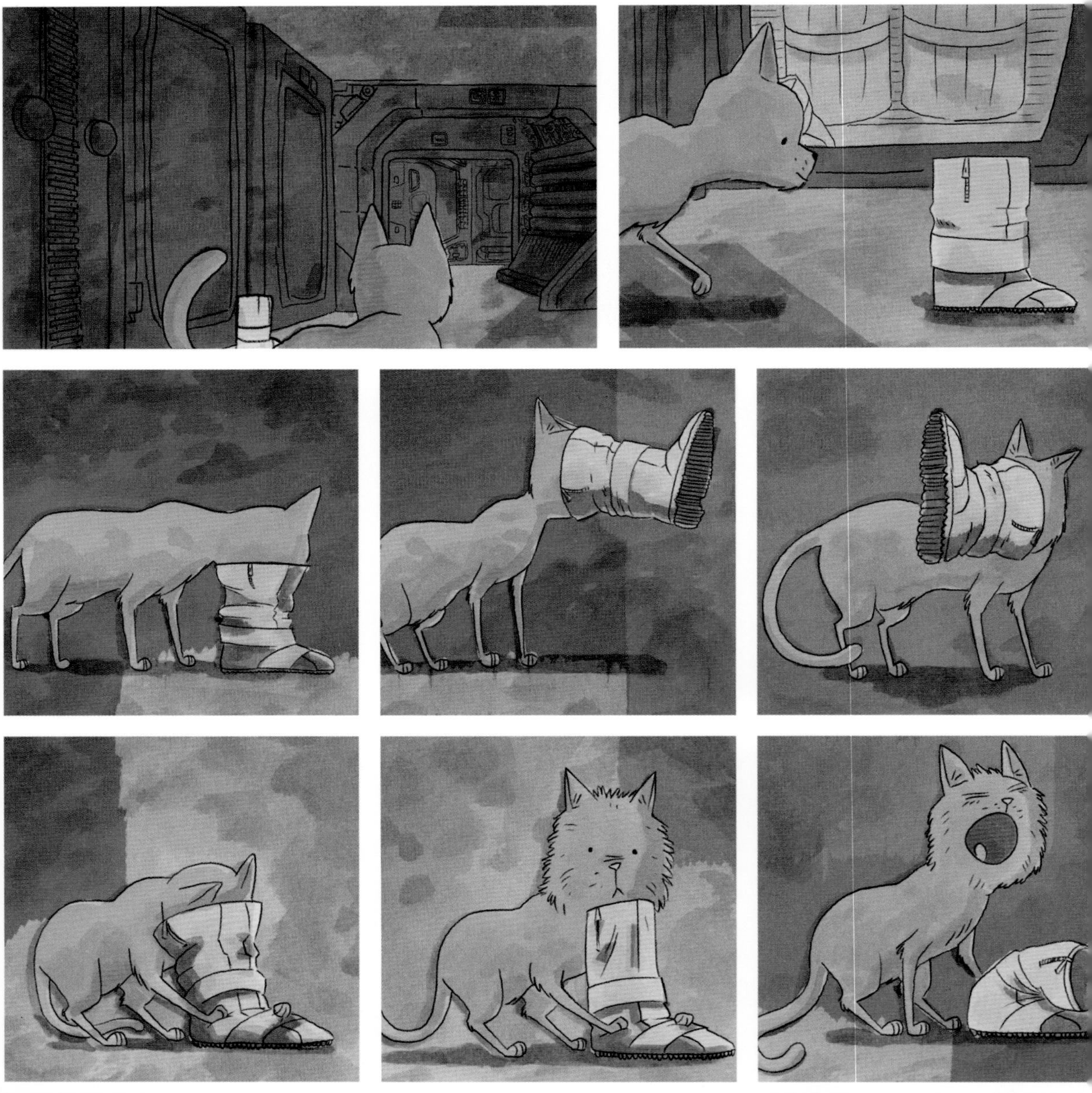

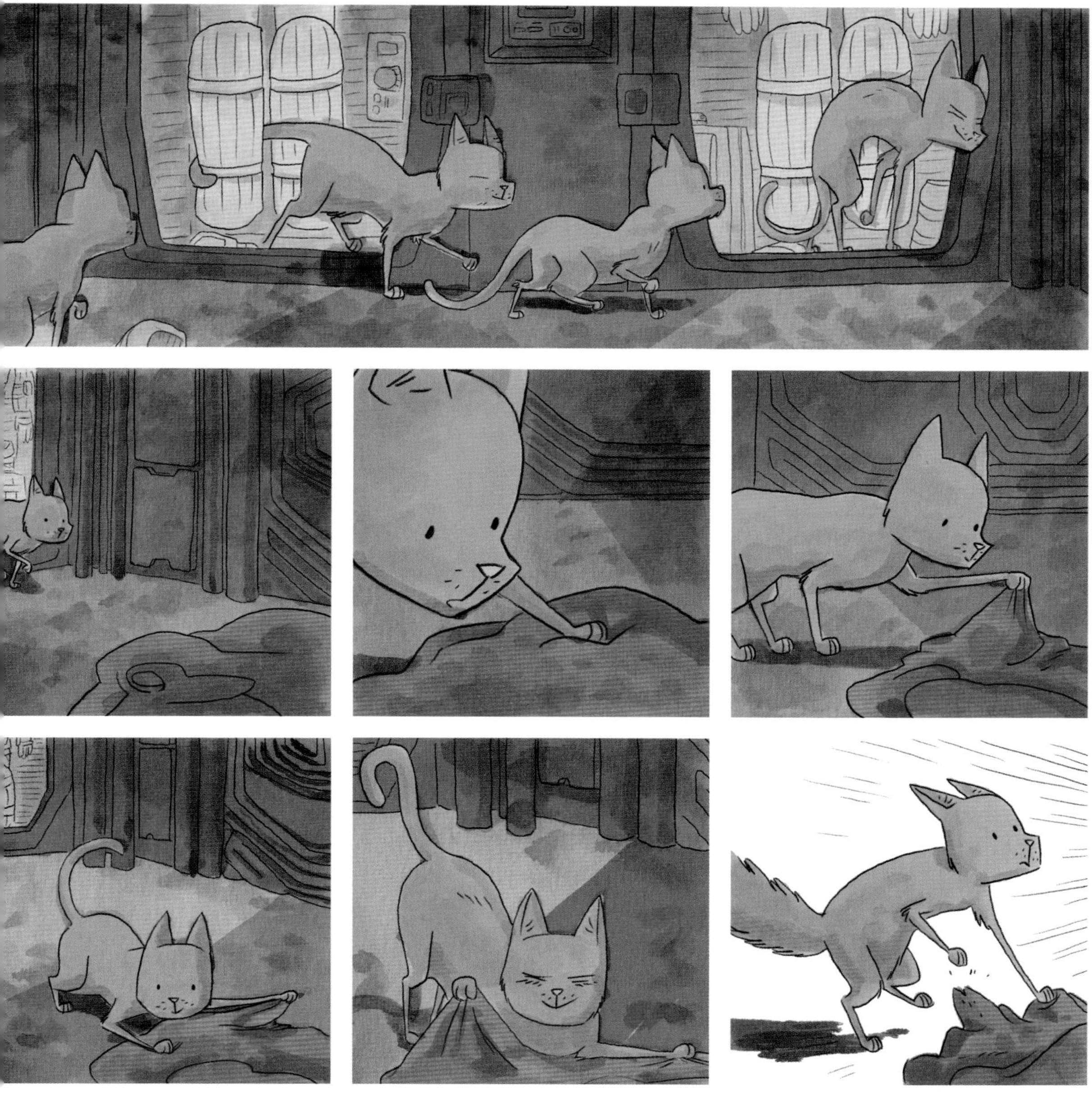

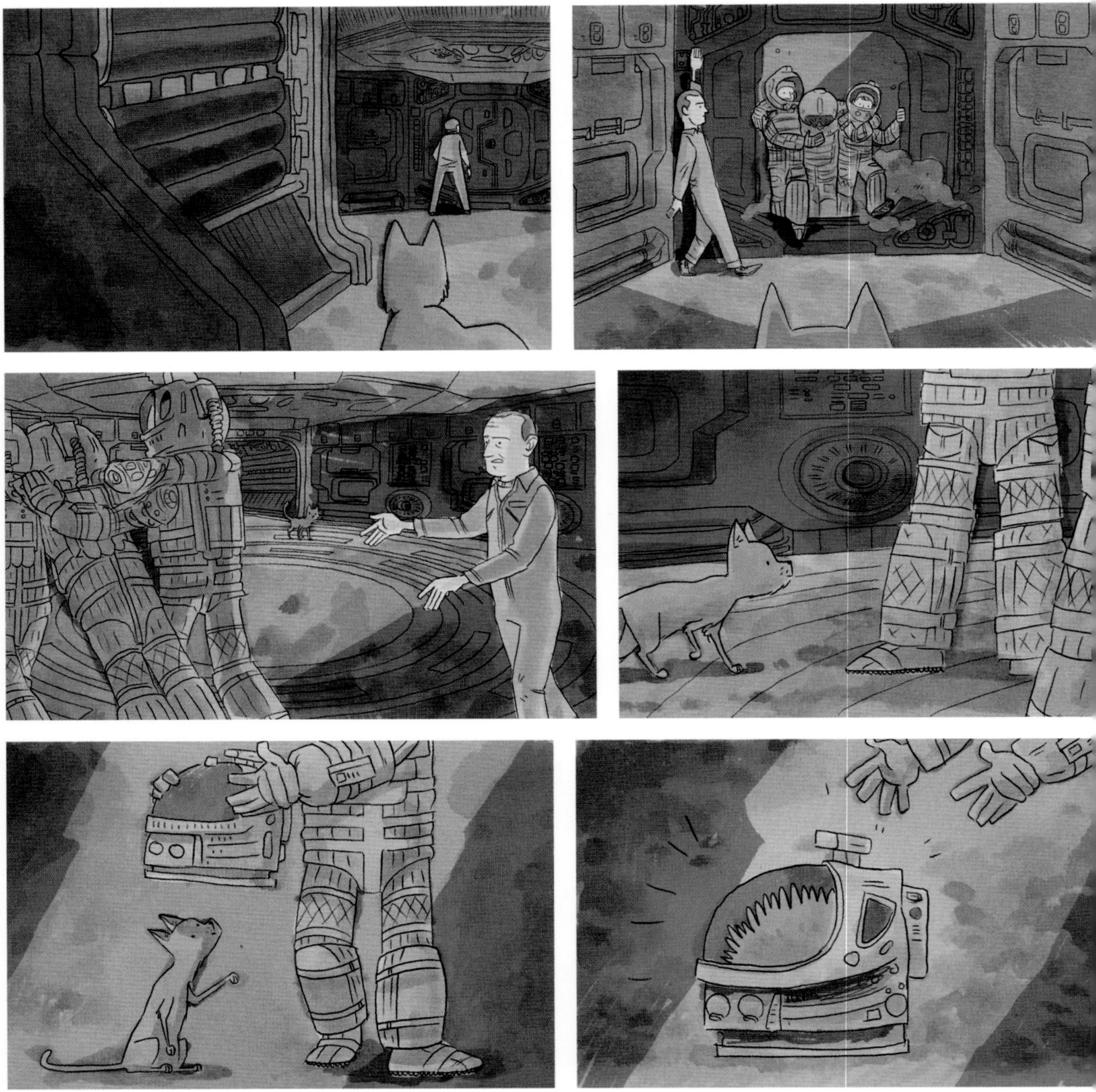

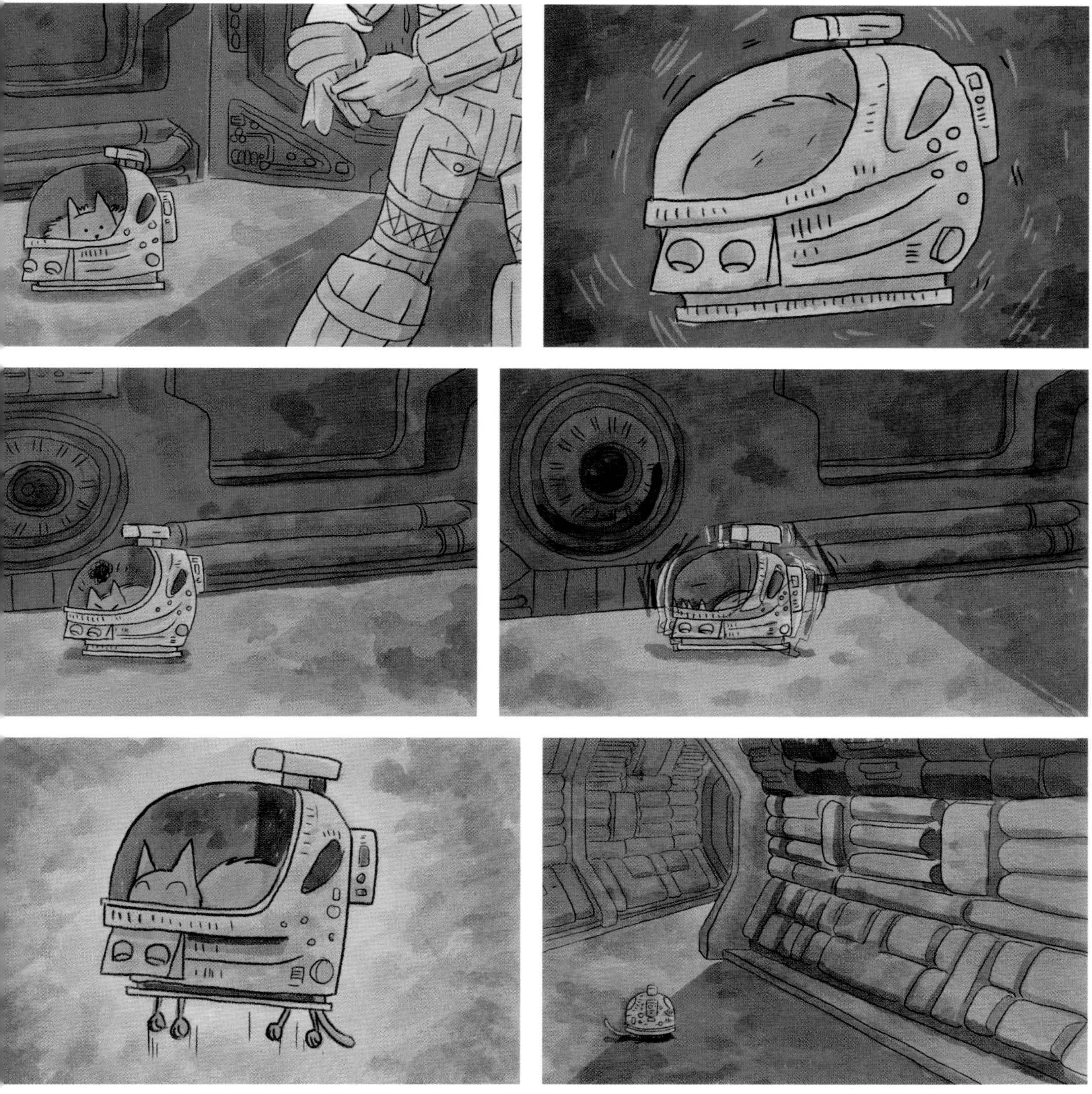

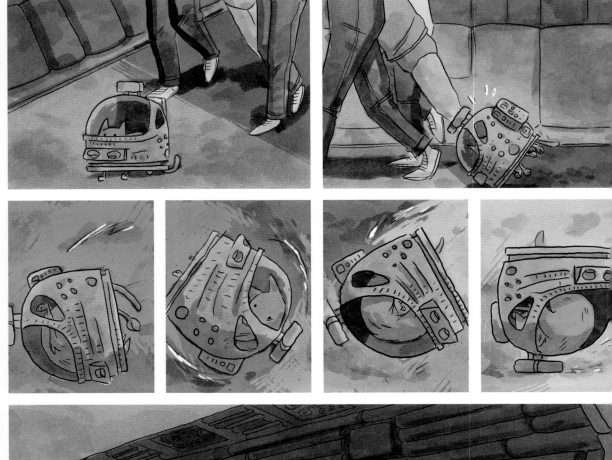

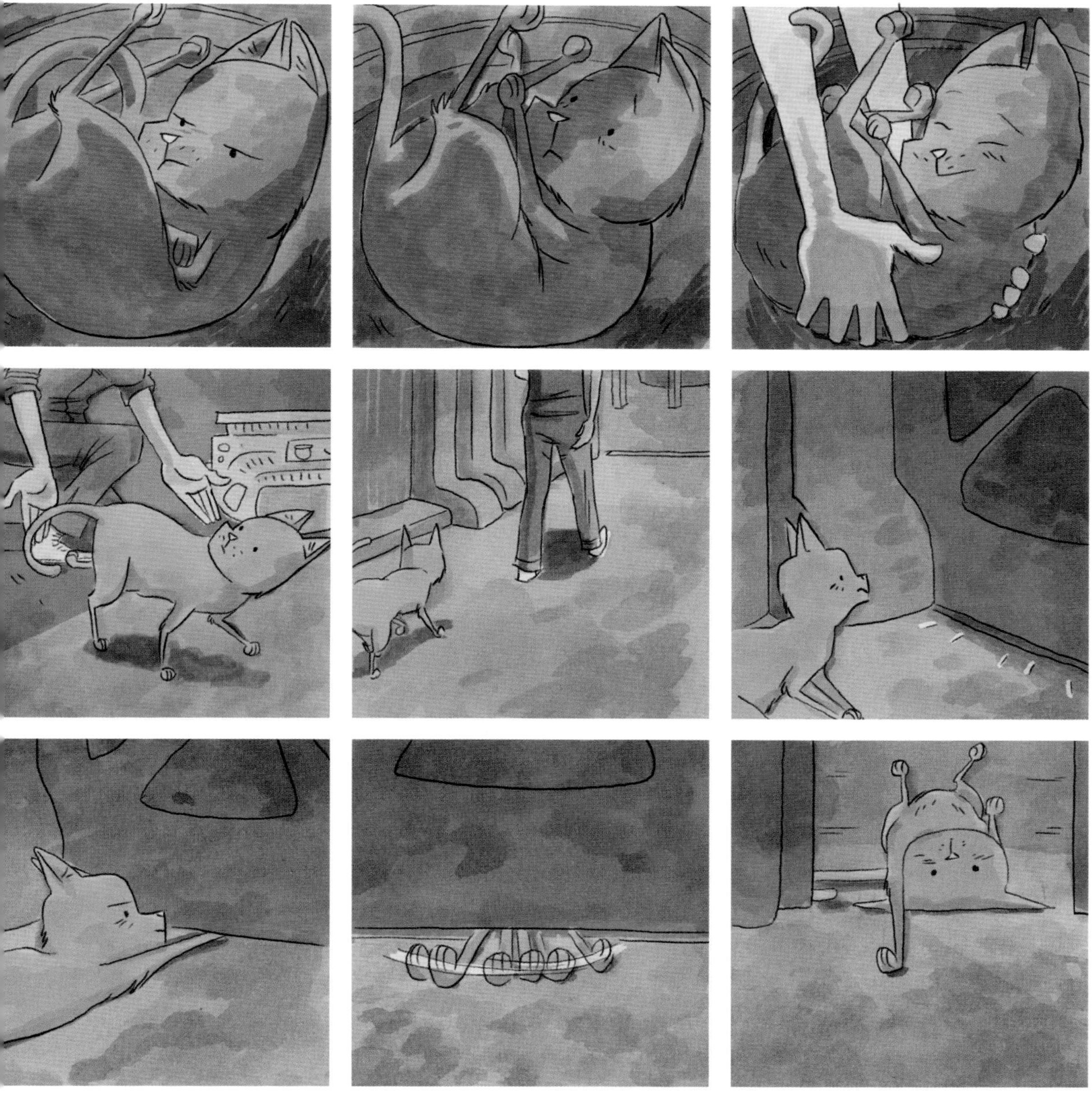

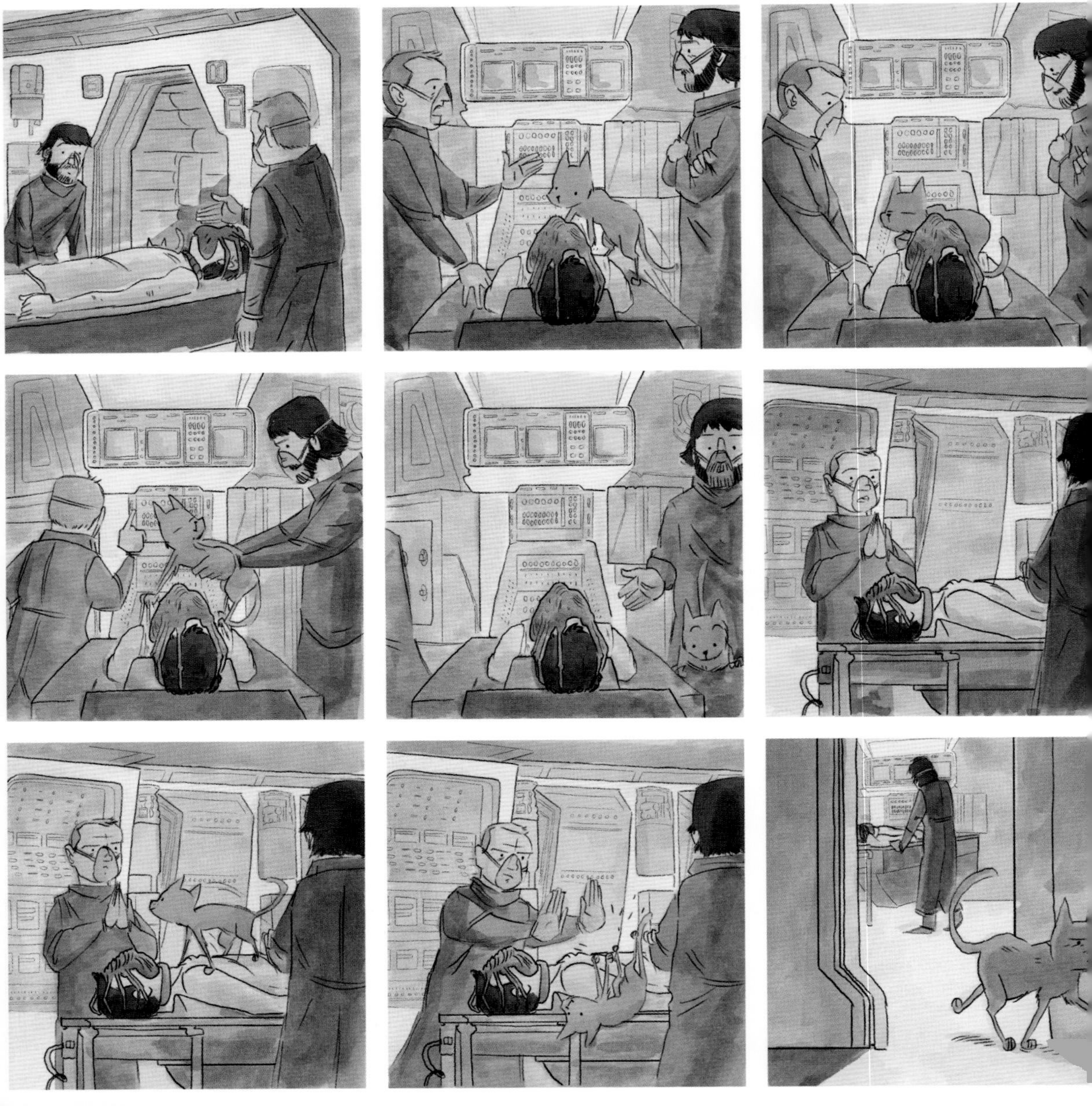

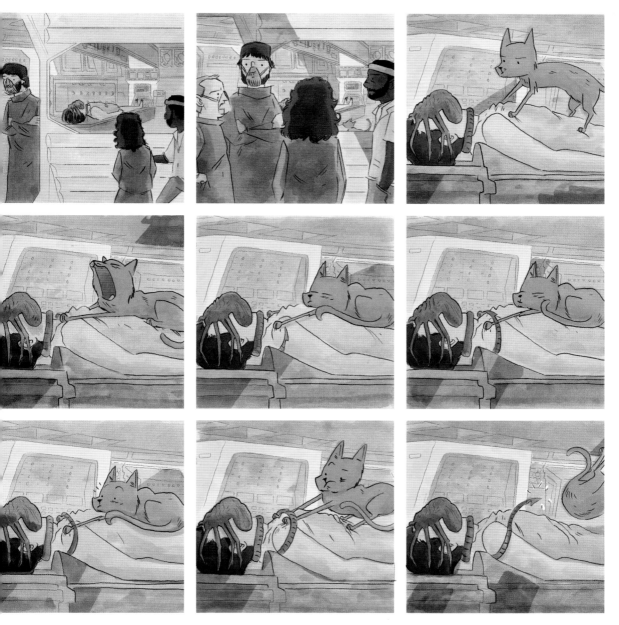

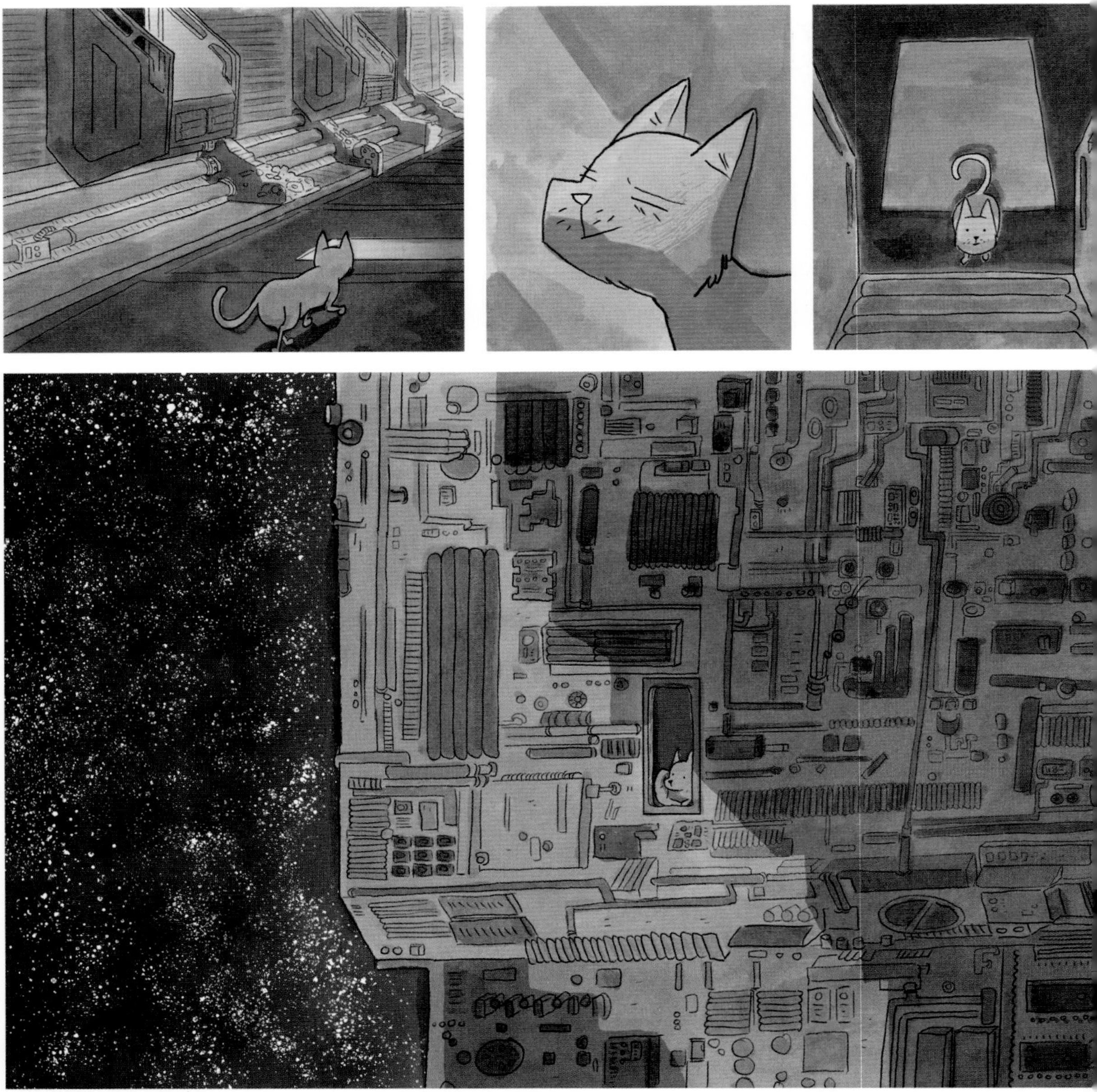

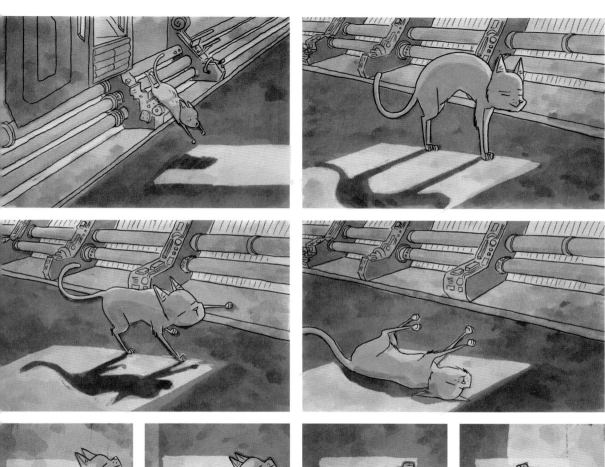
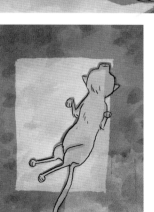

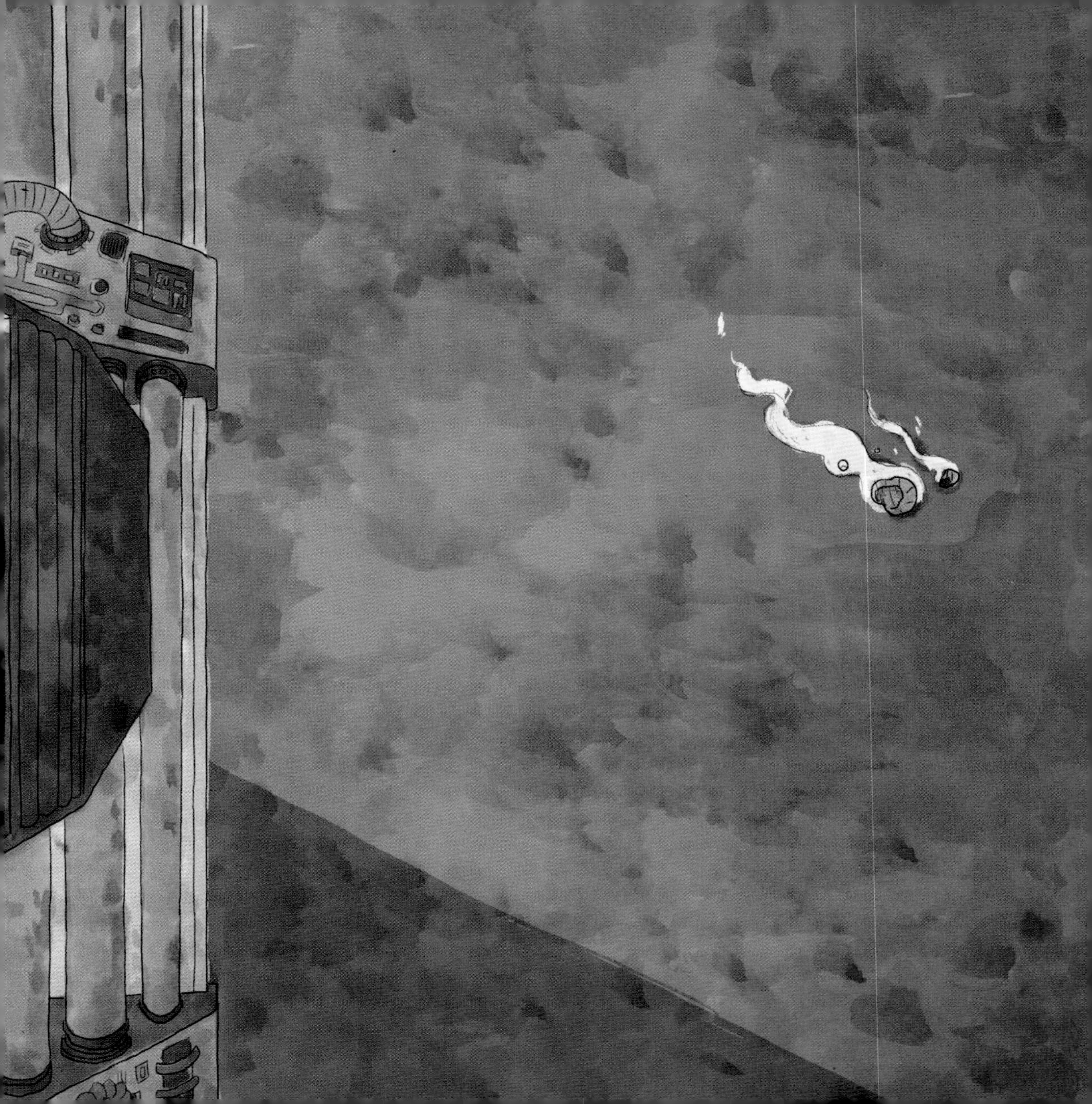

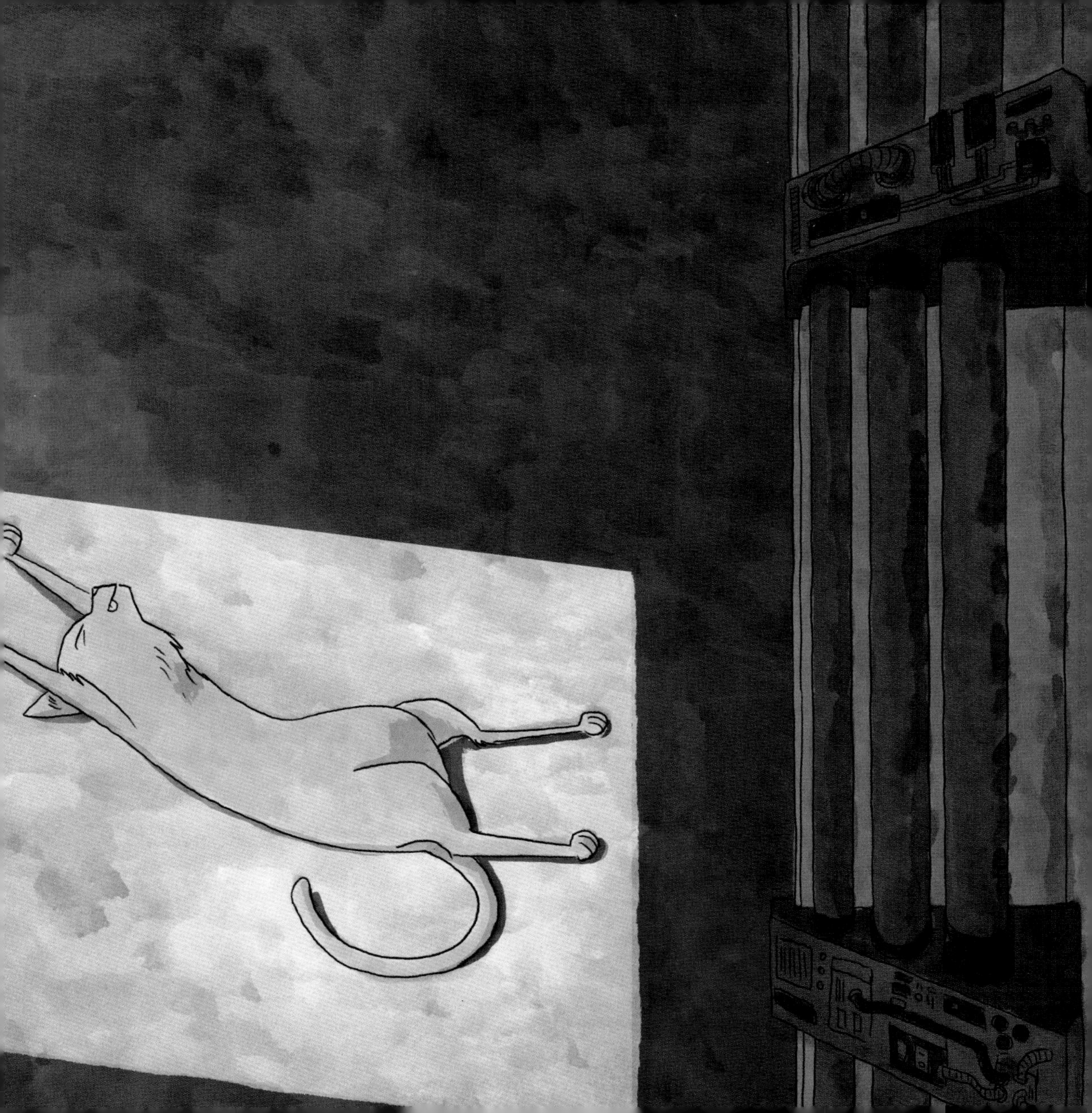

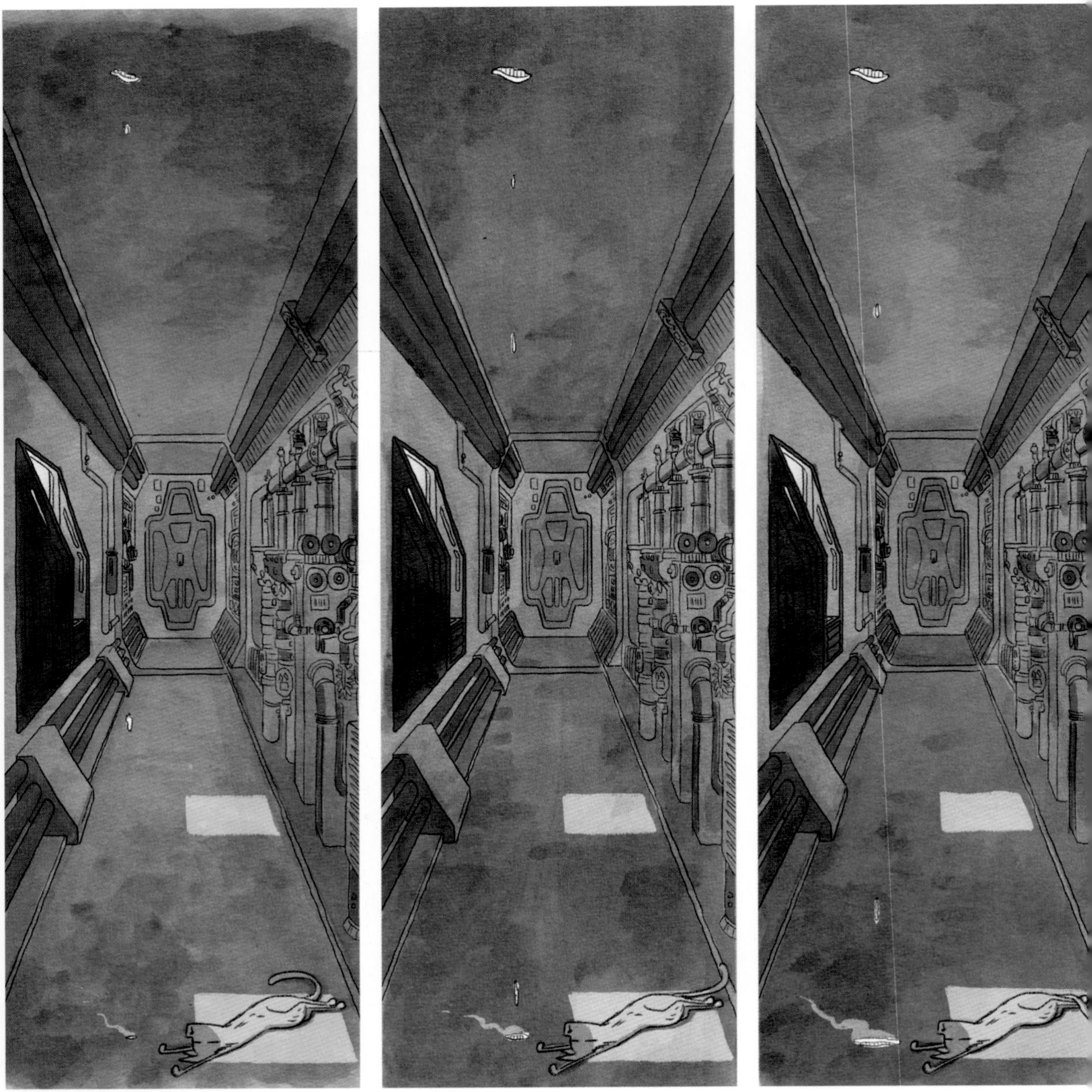

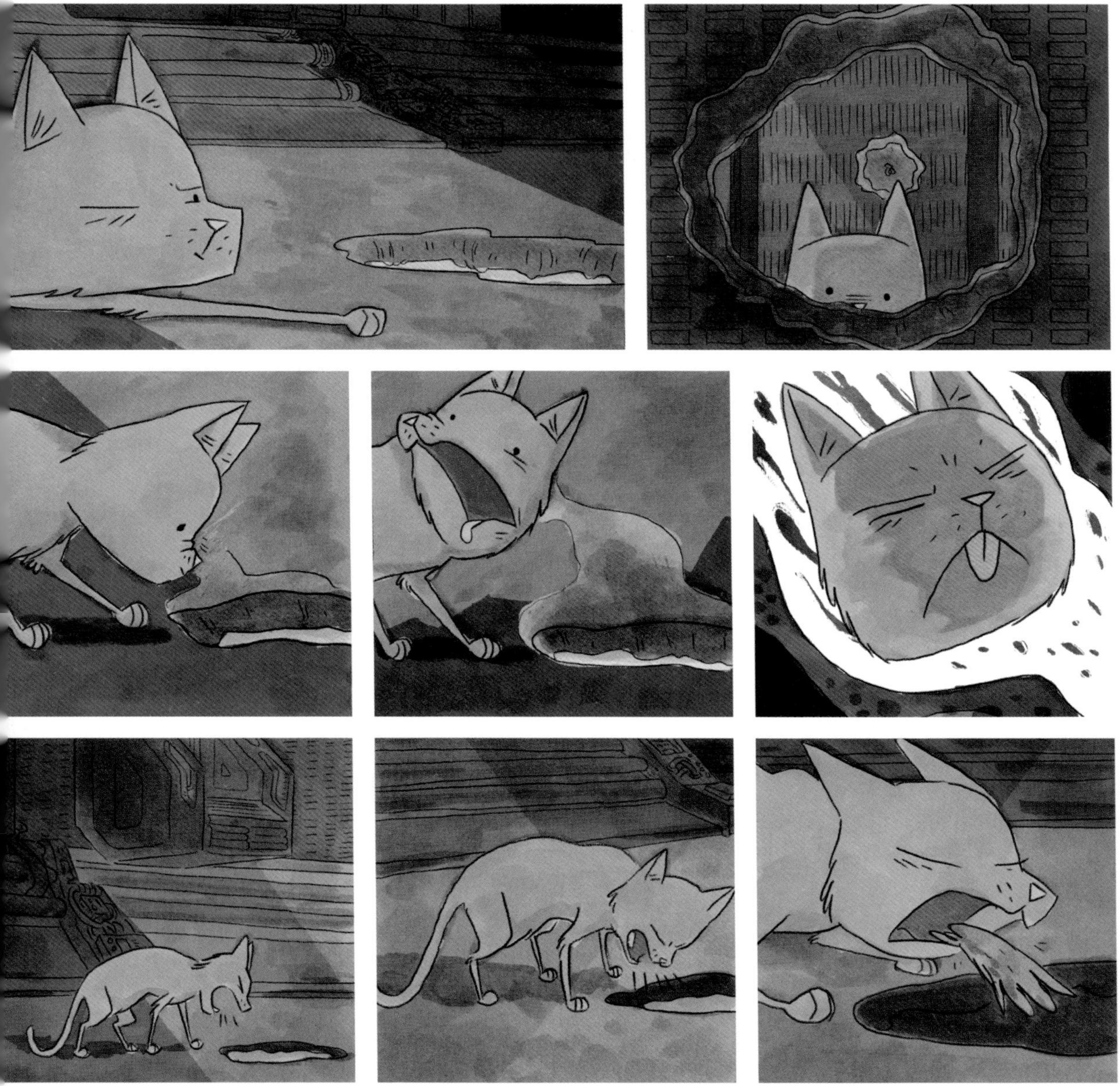

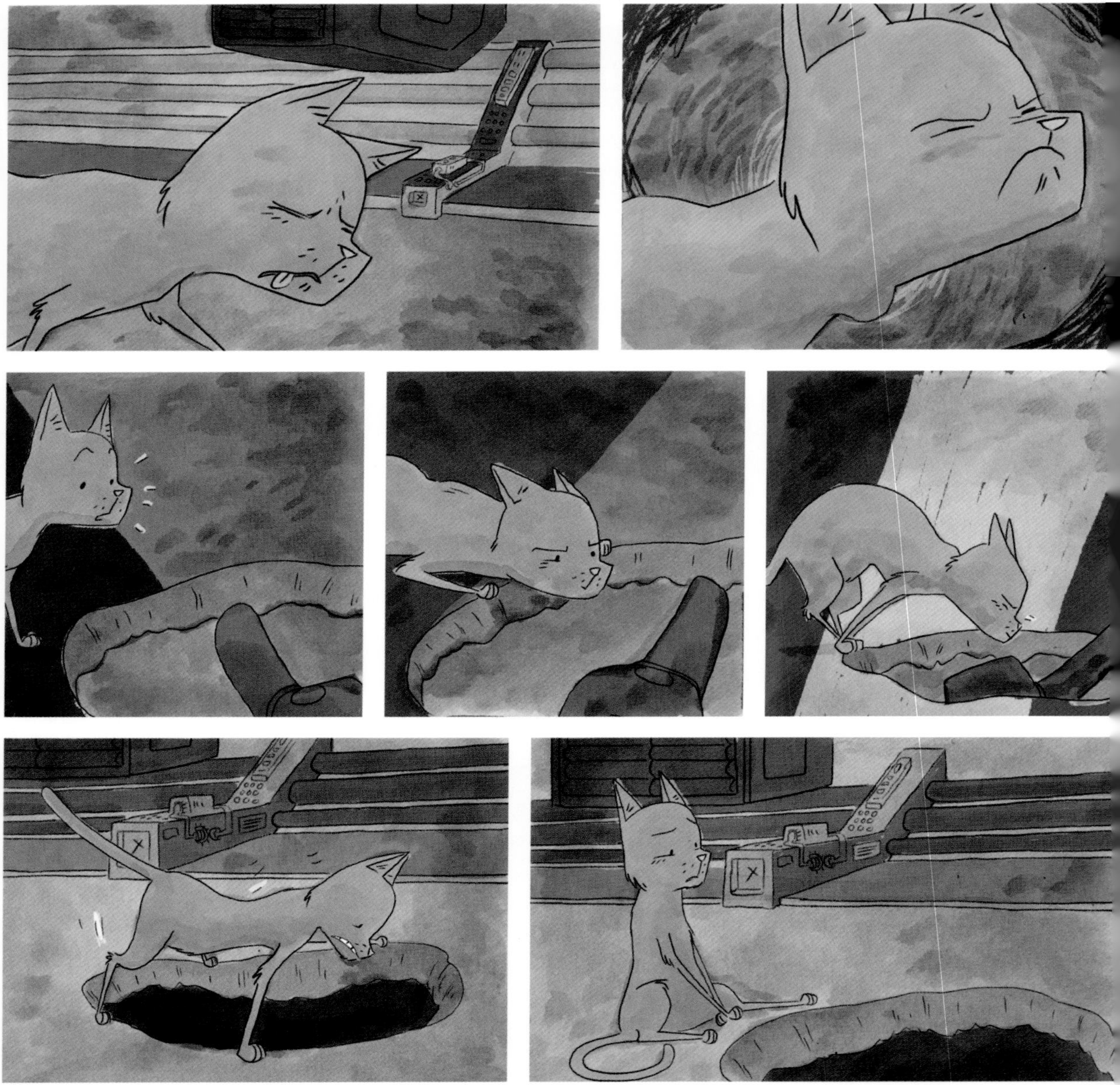

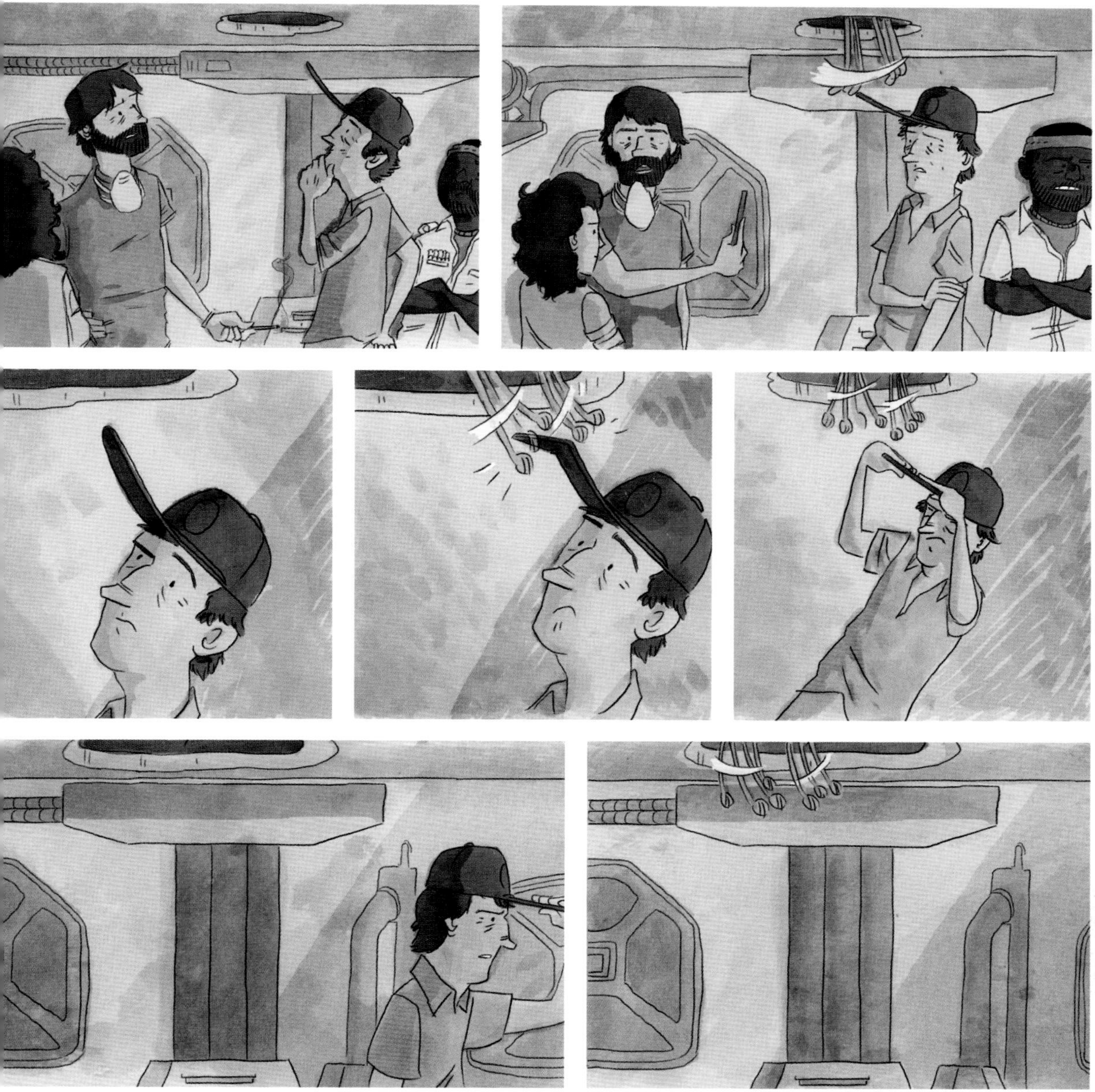

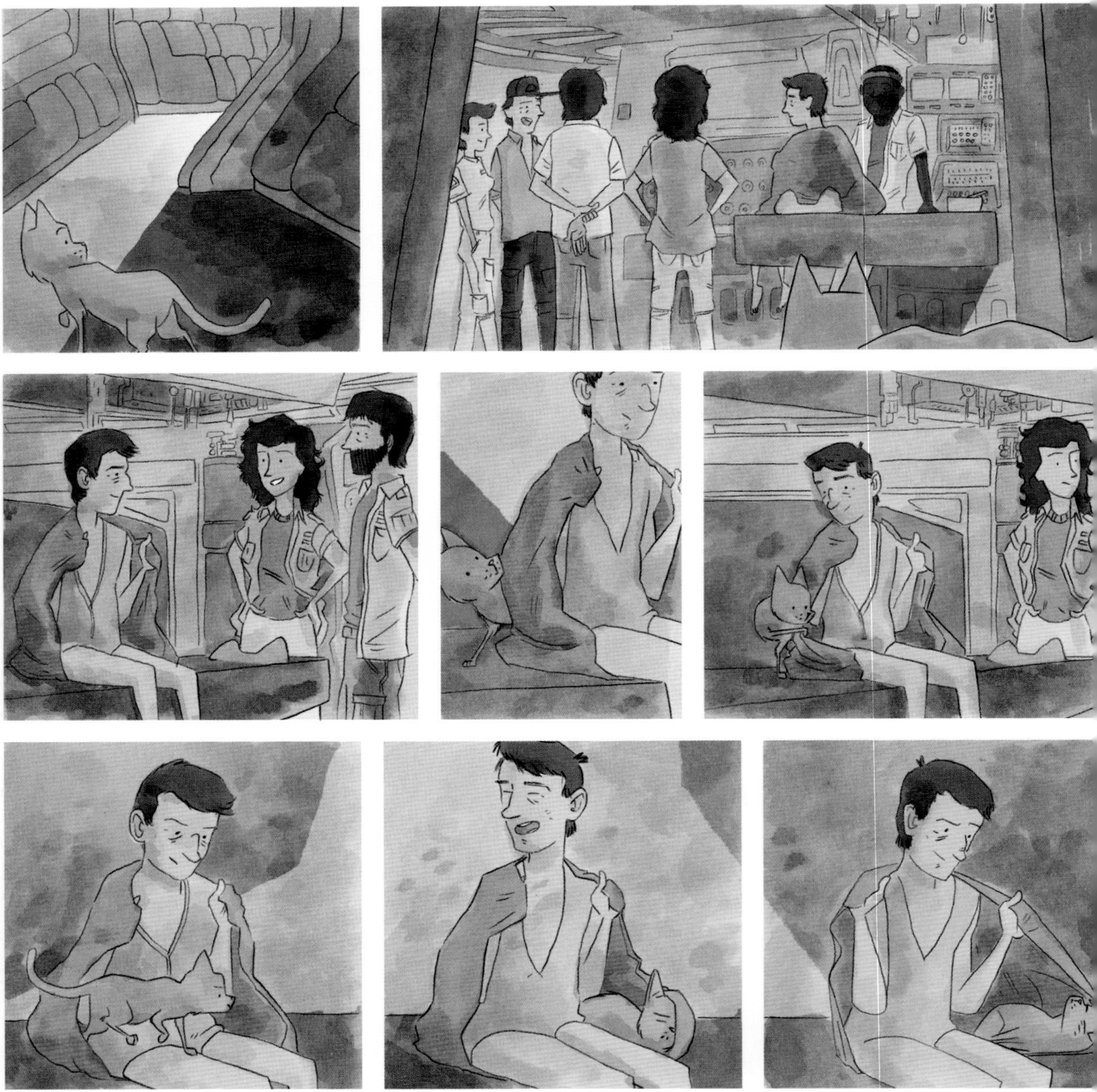

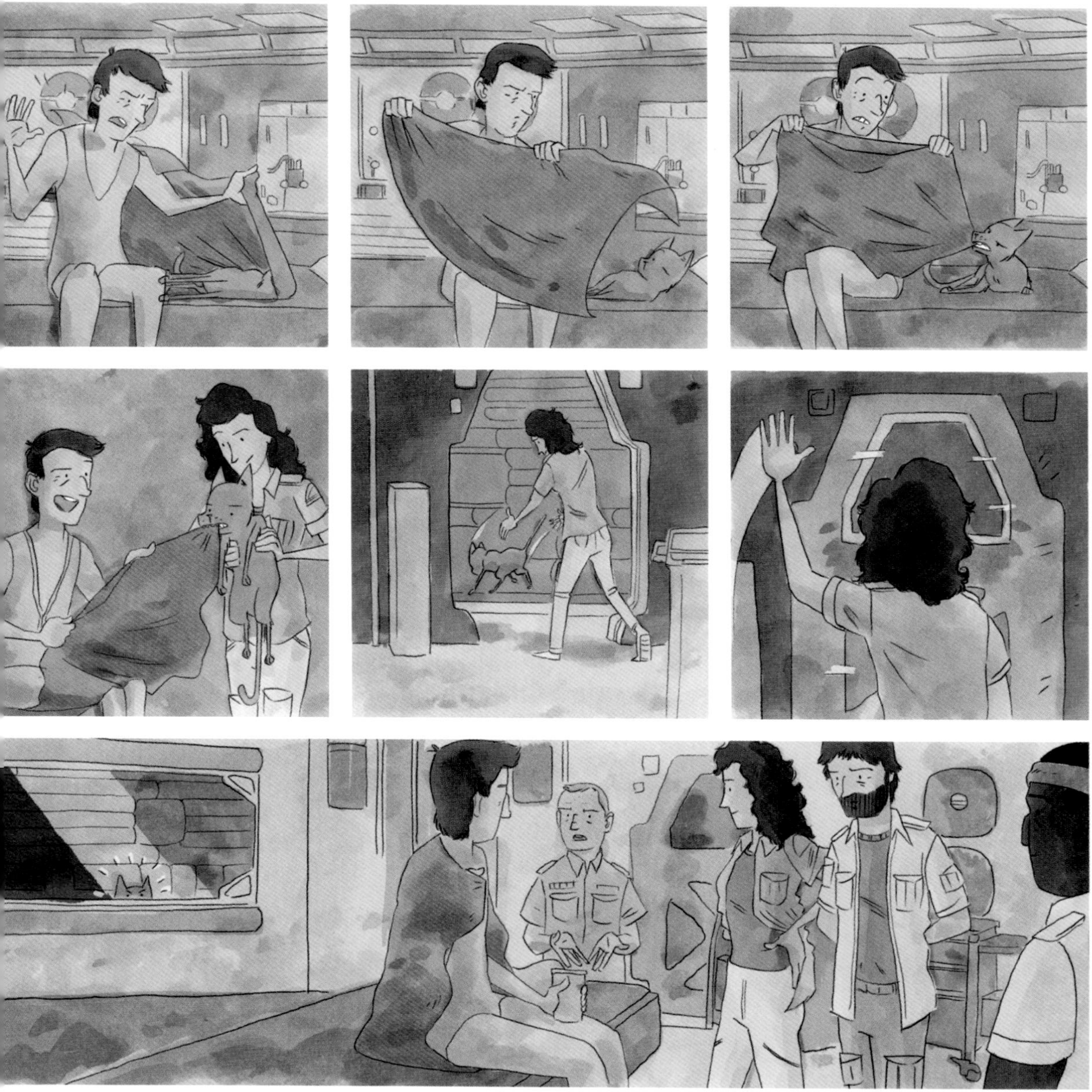

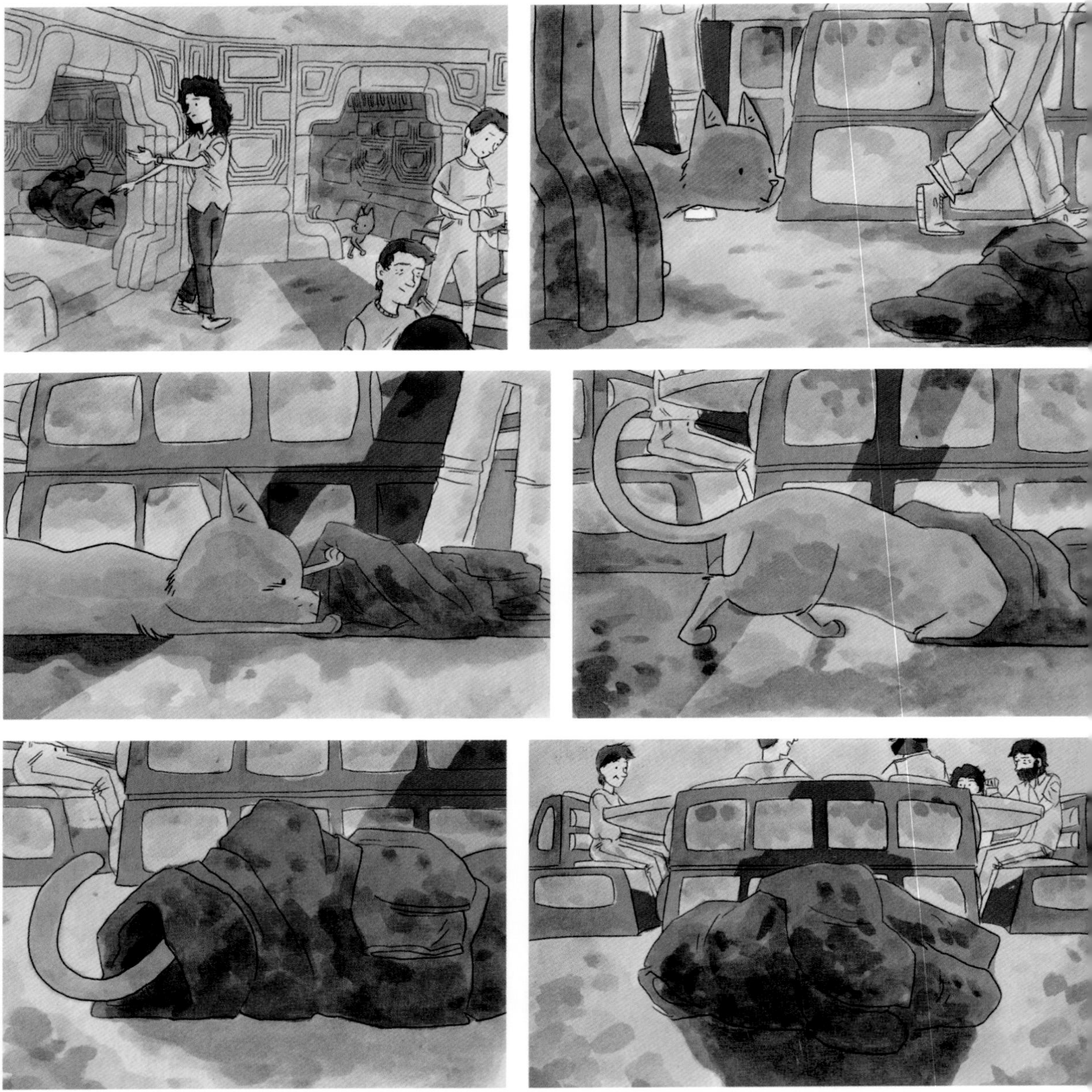

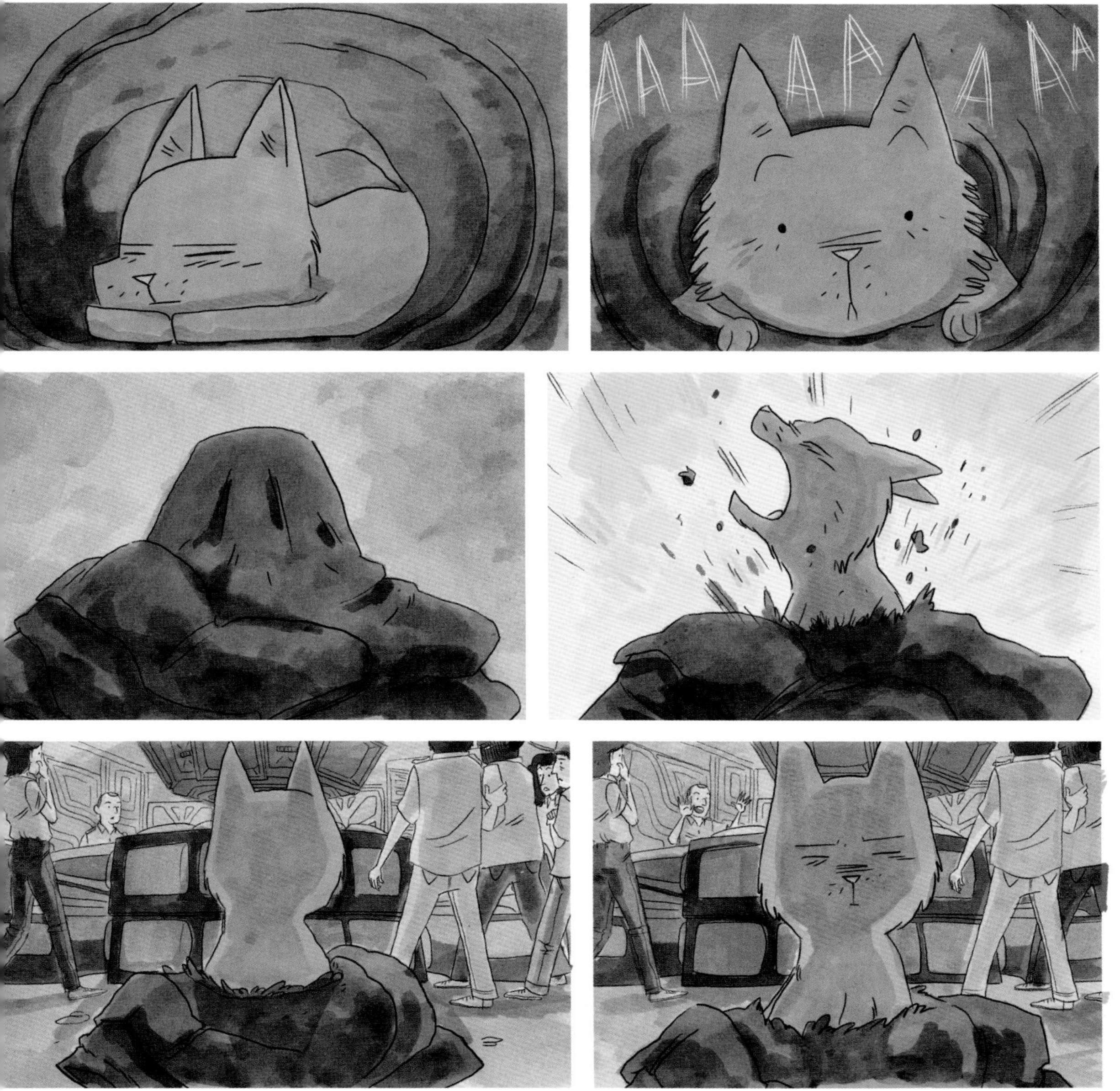
AAAAAAAA

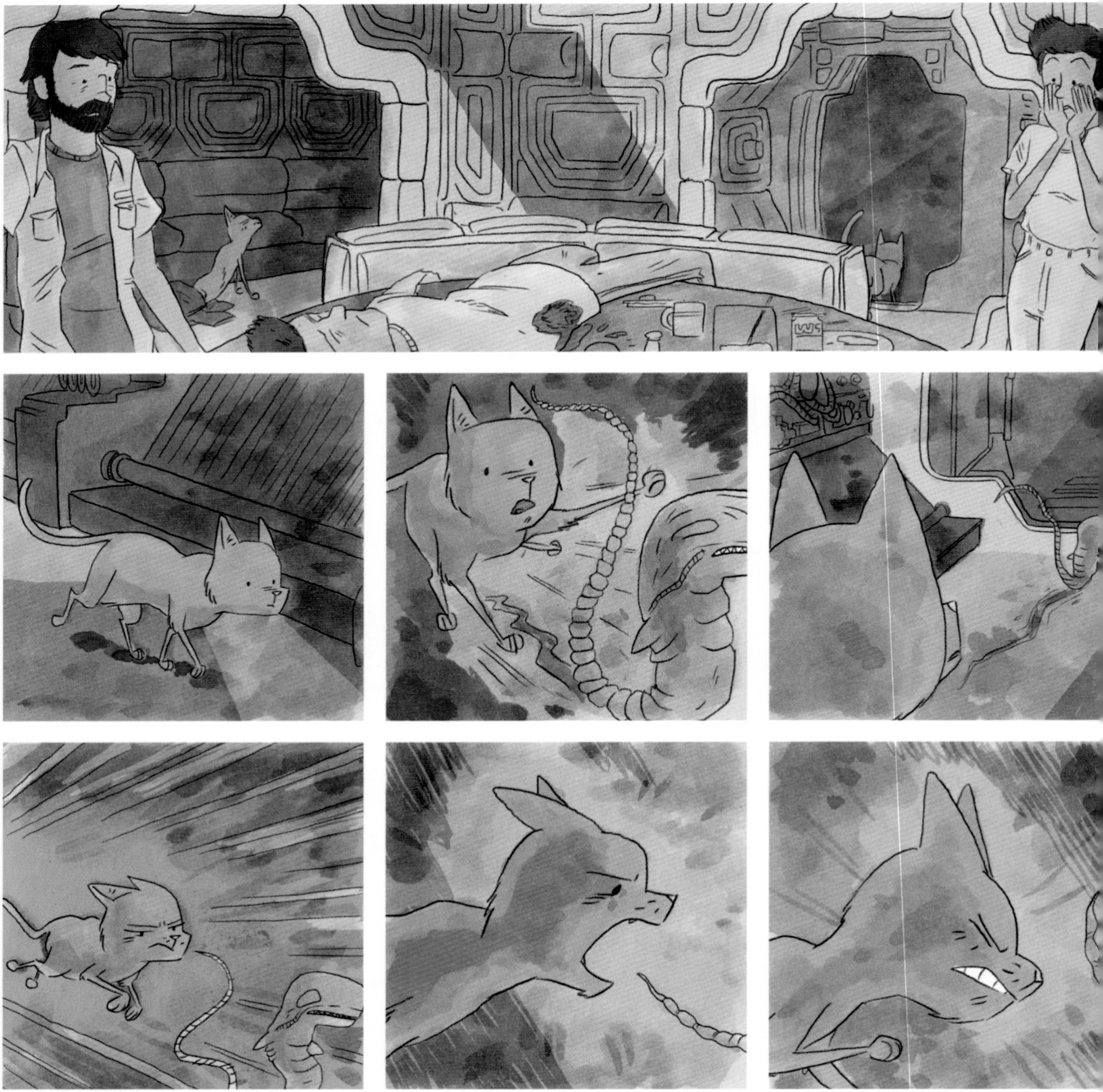

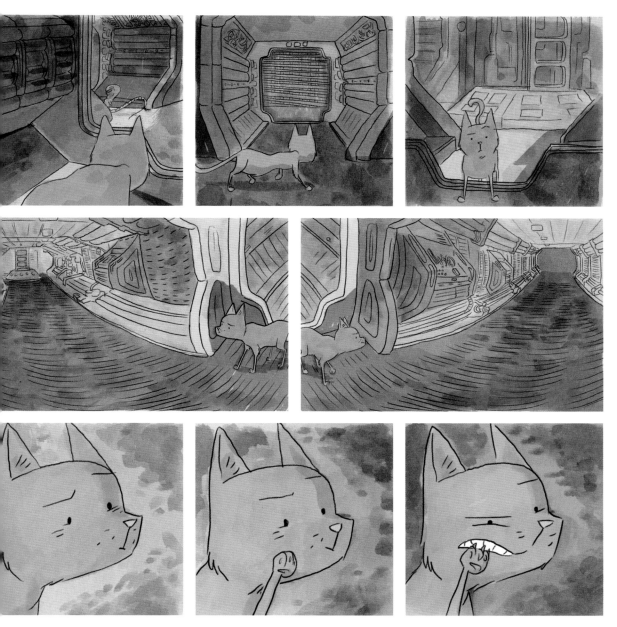

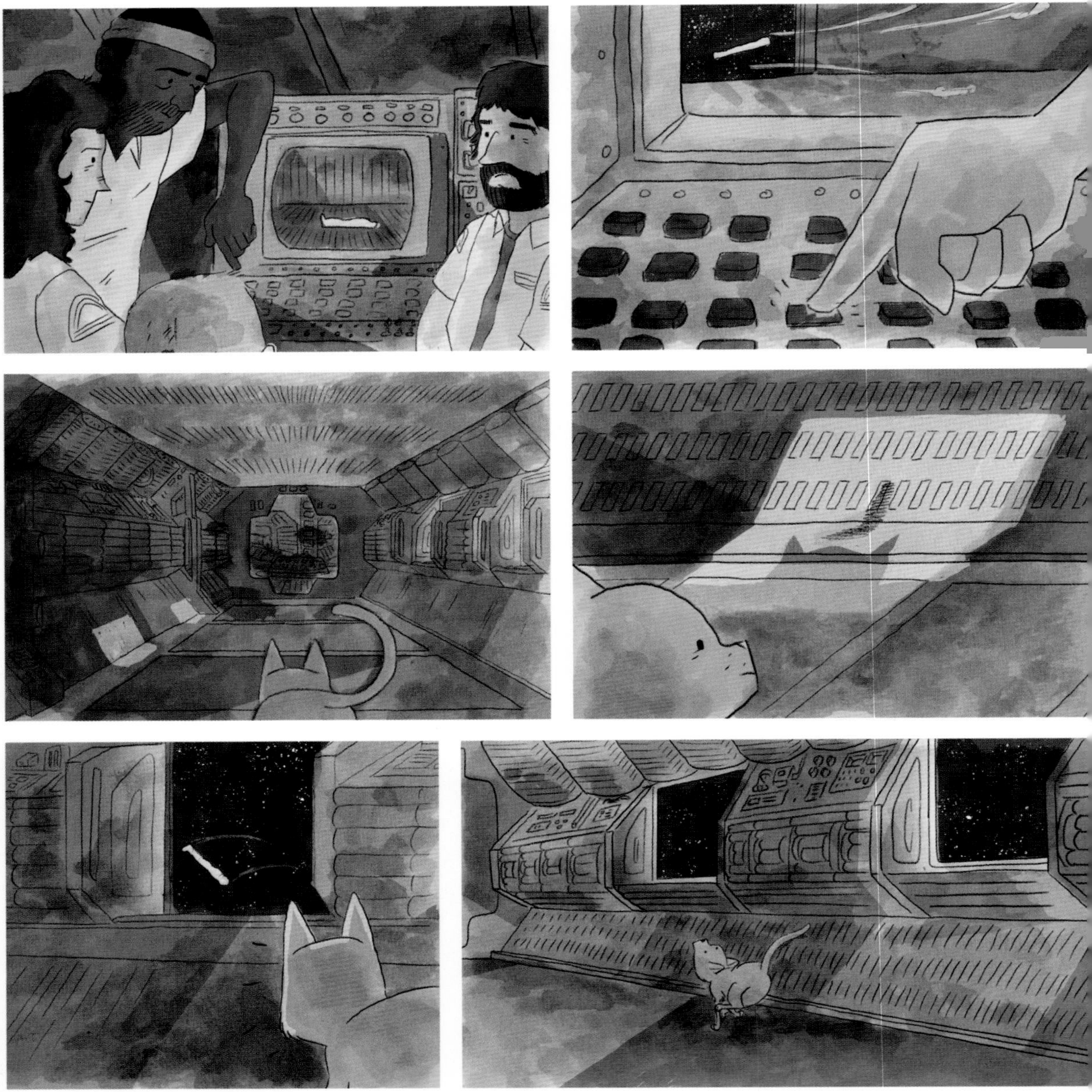

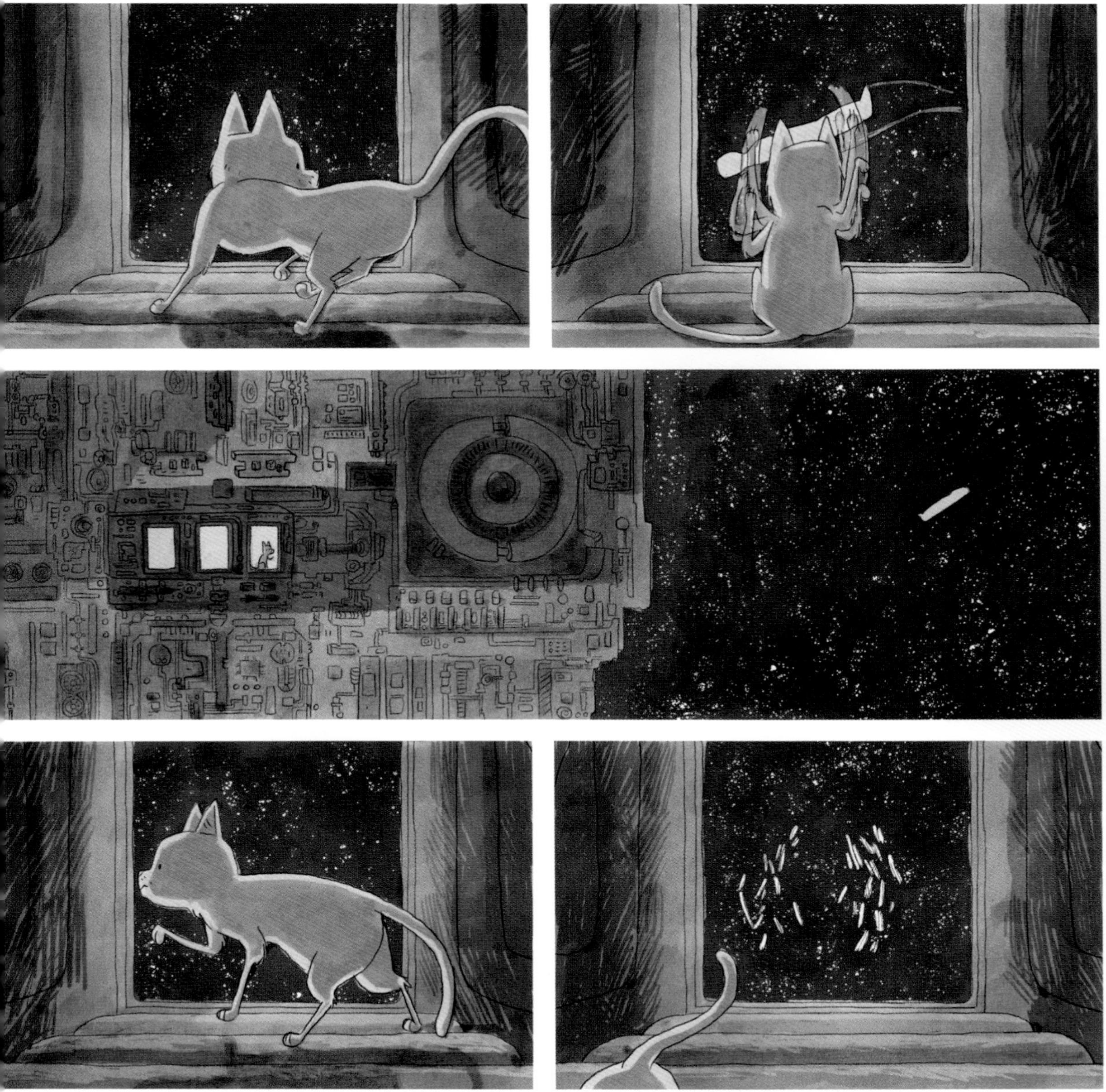

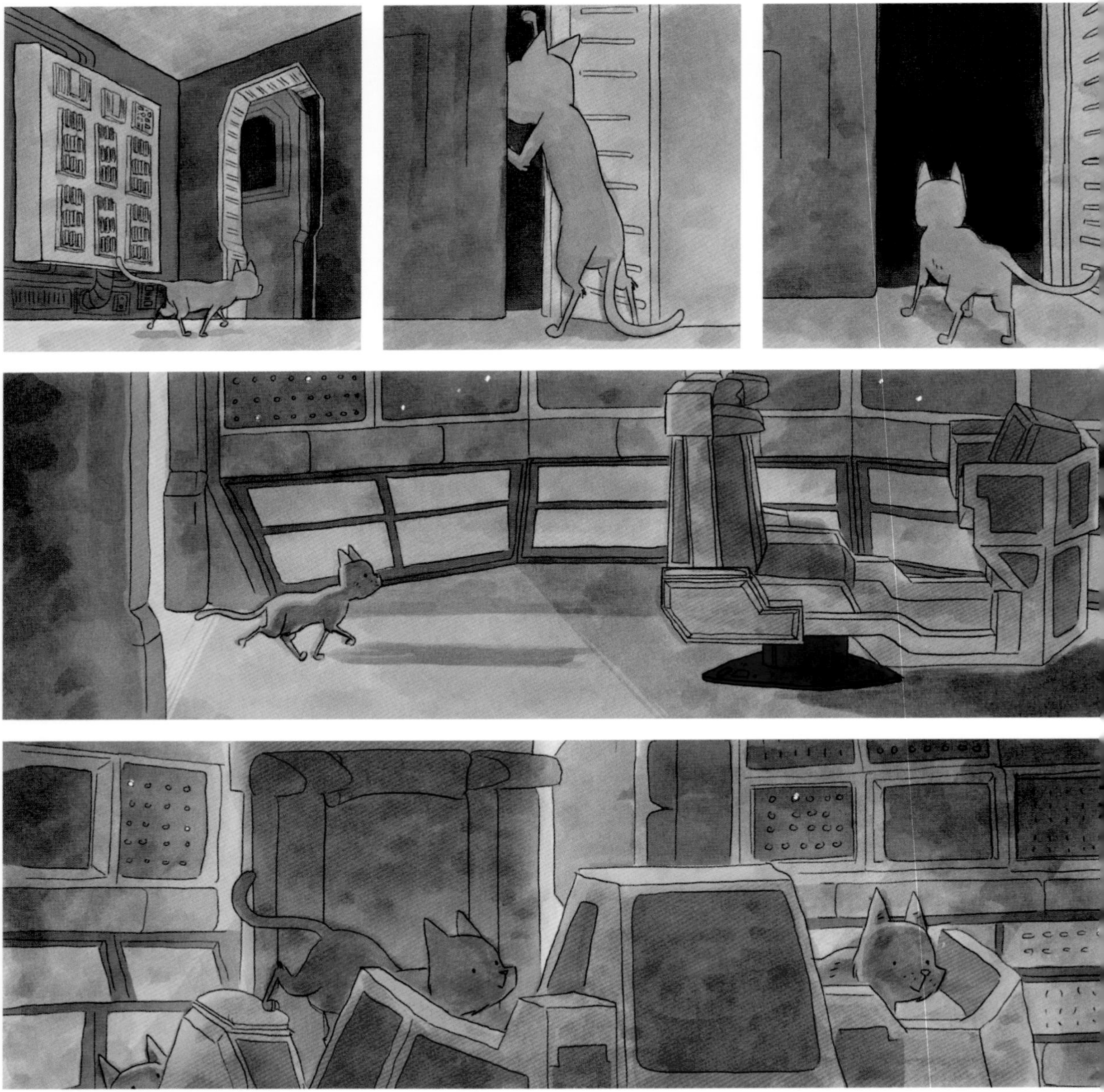

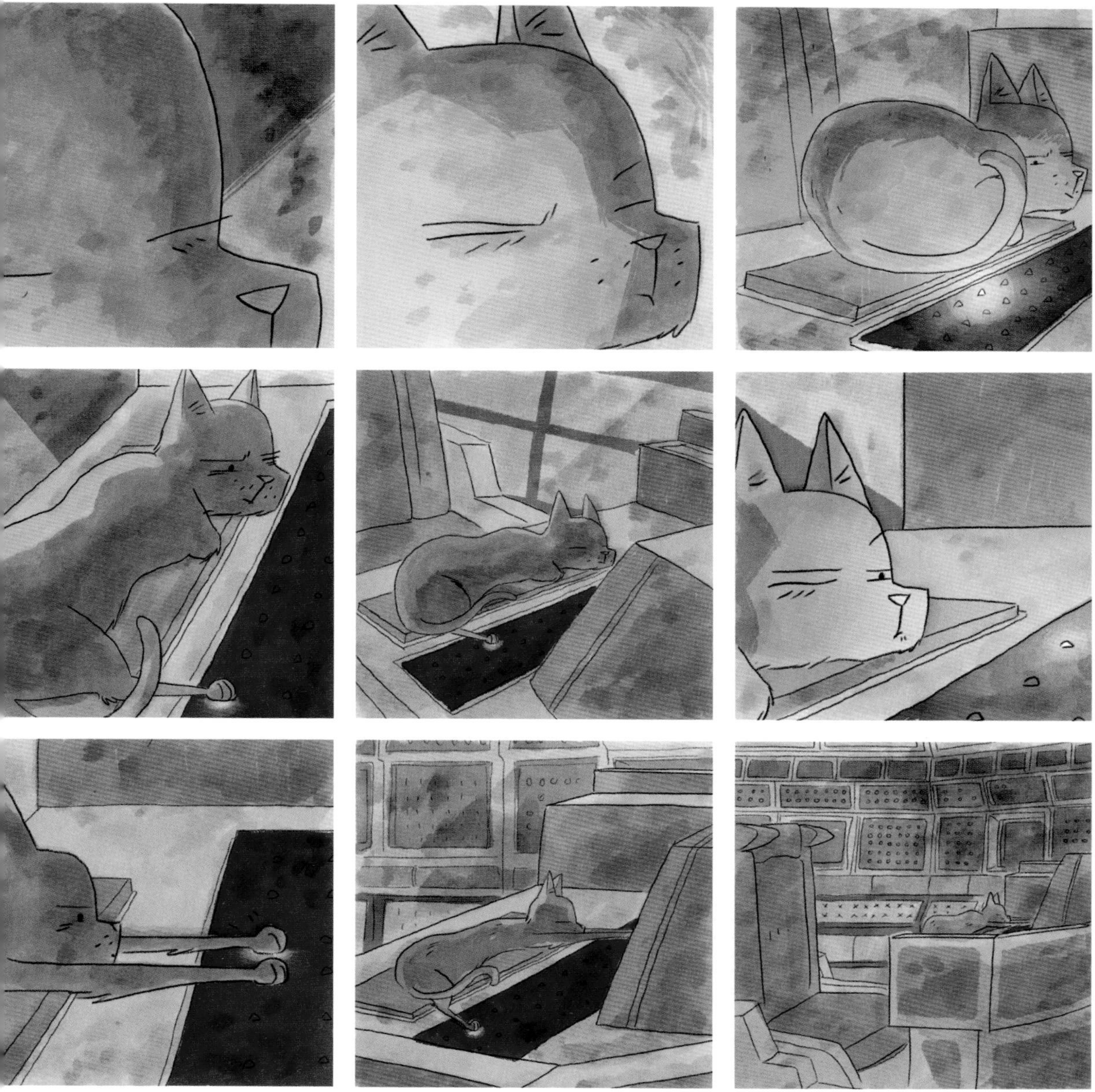

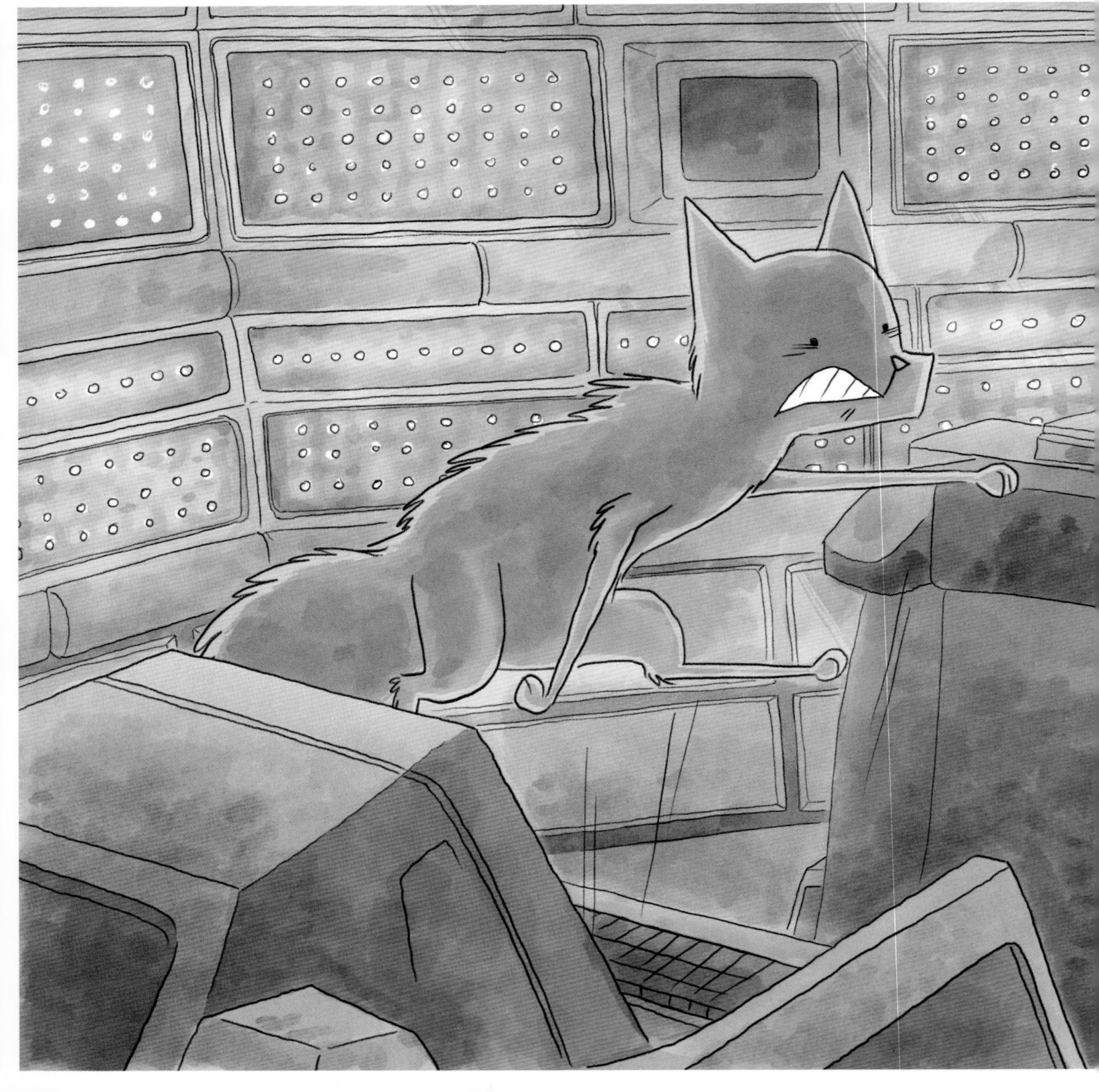

  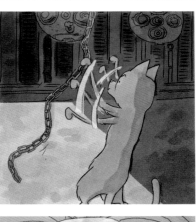

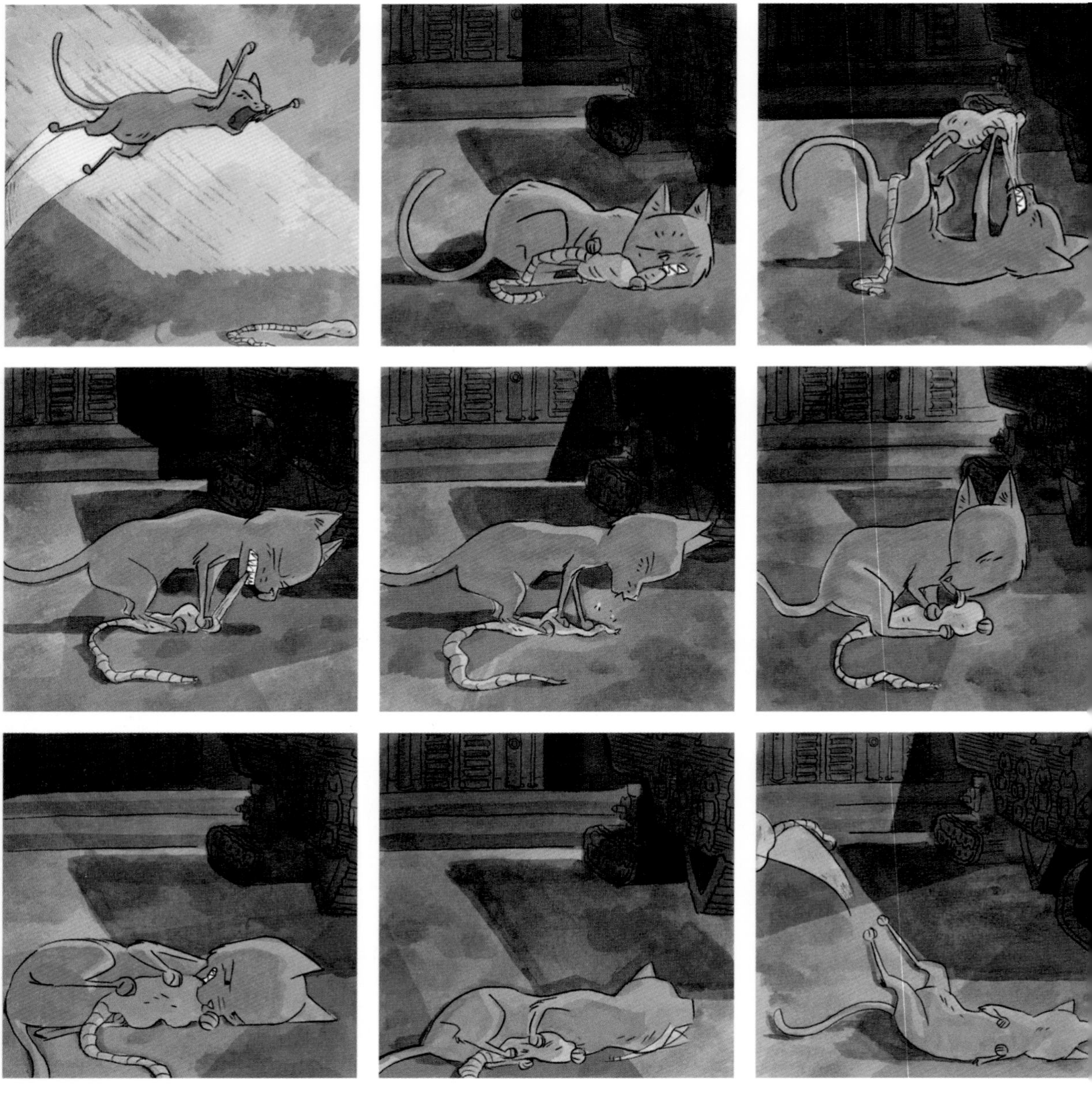

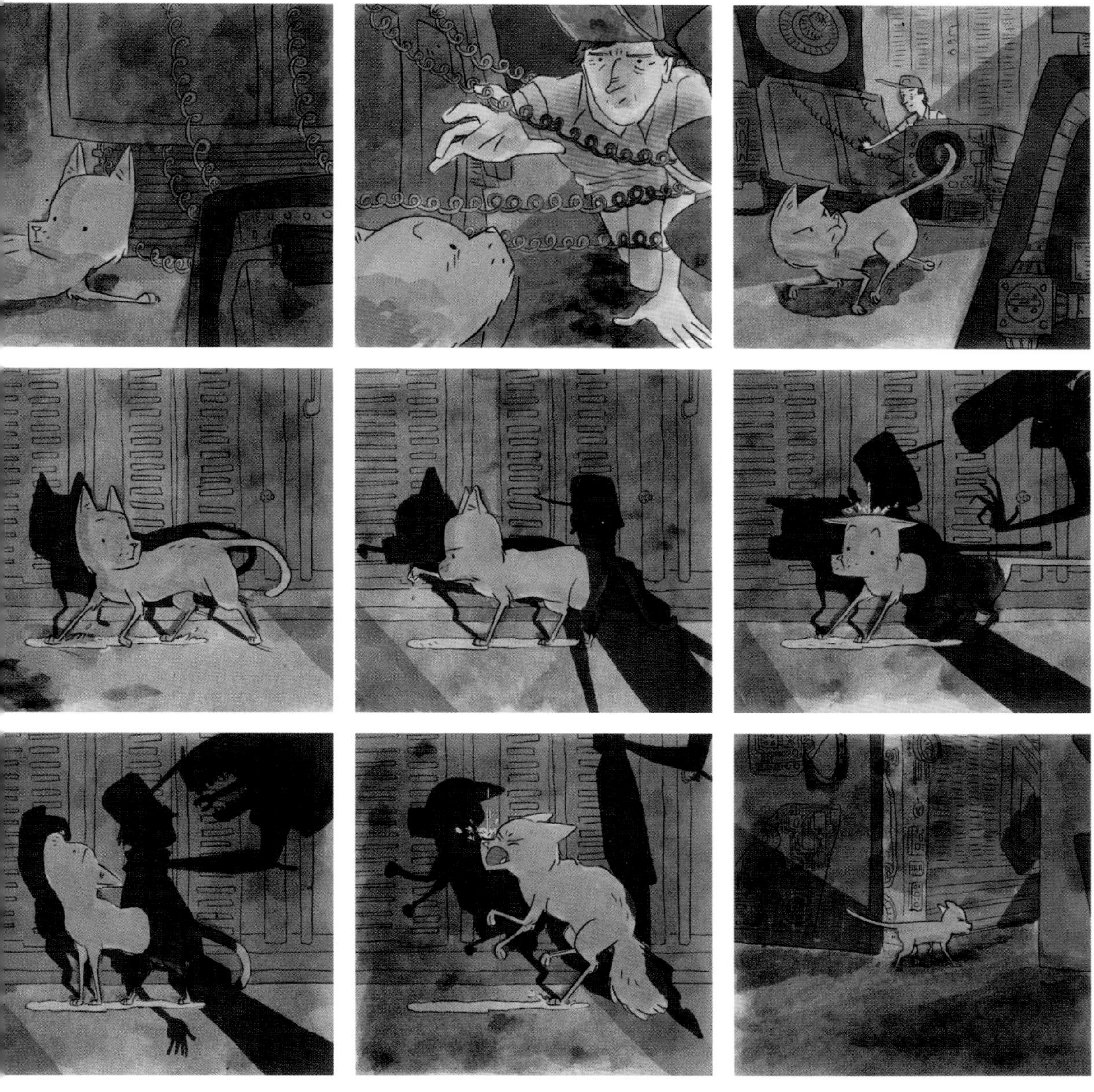

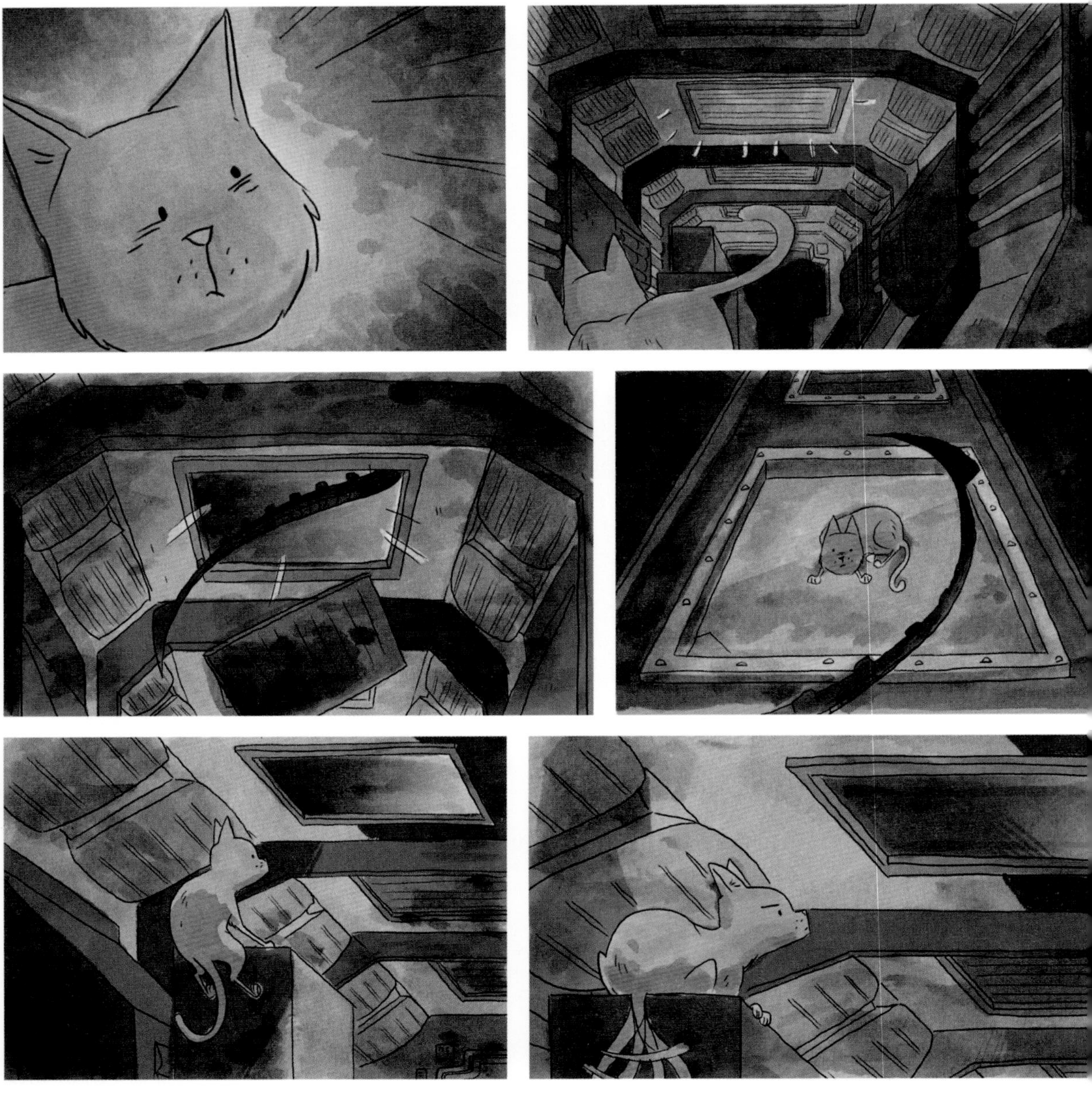

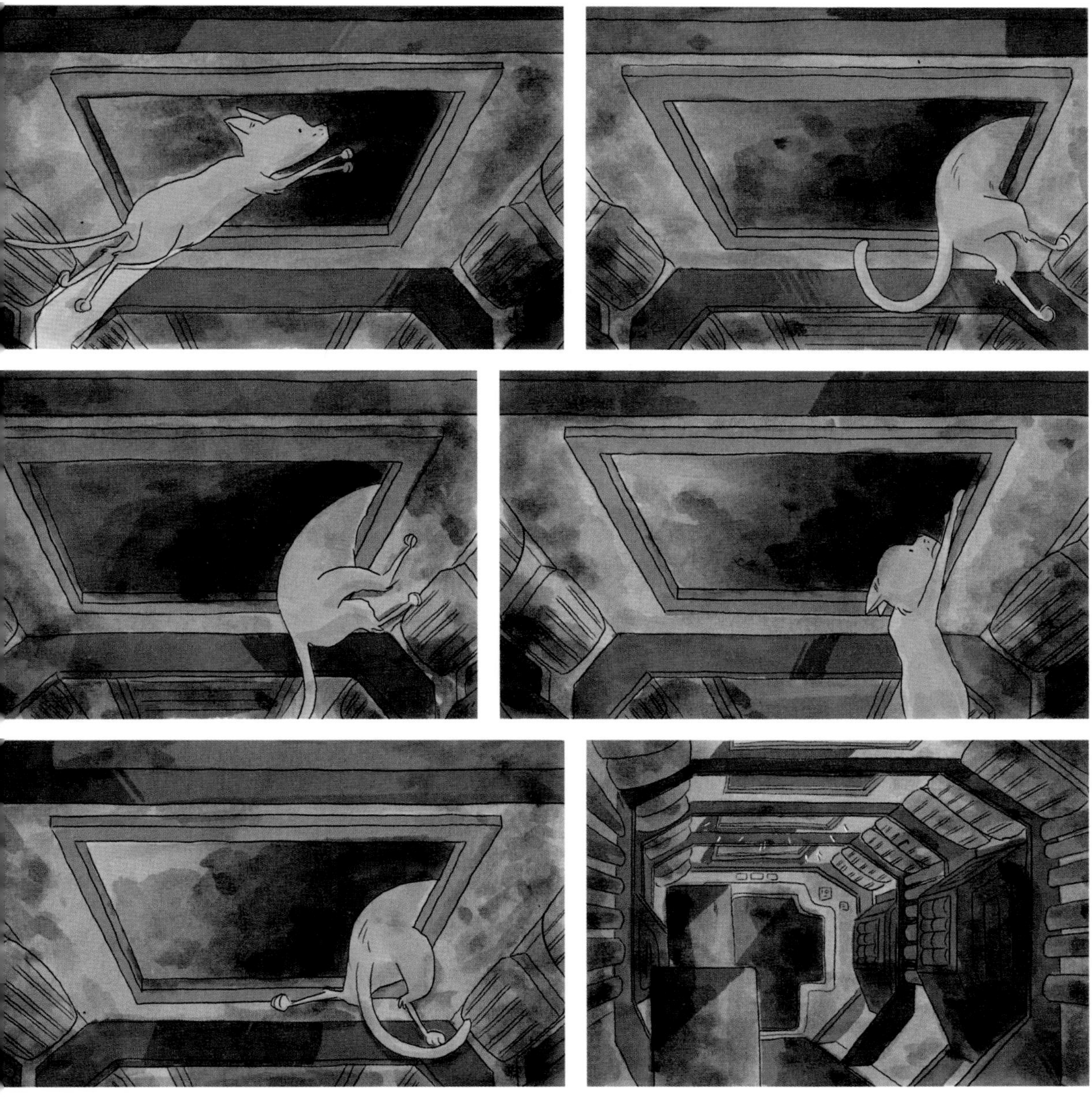

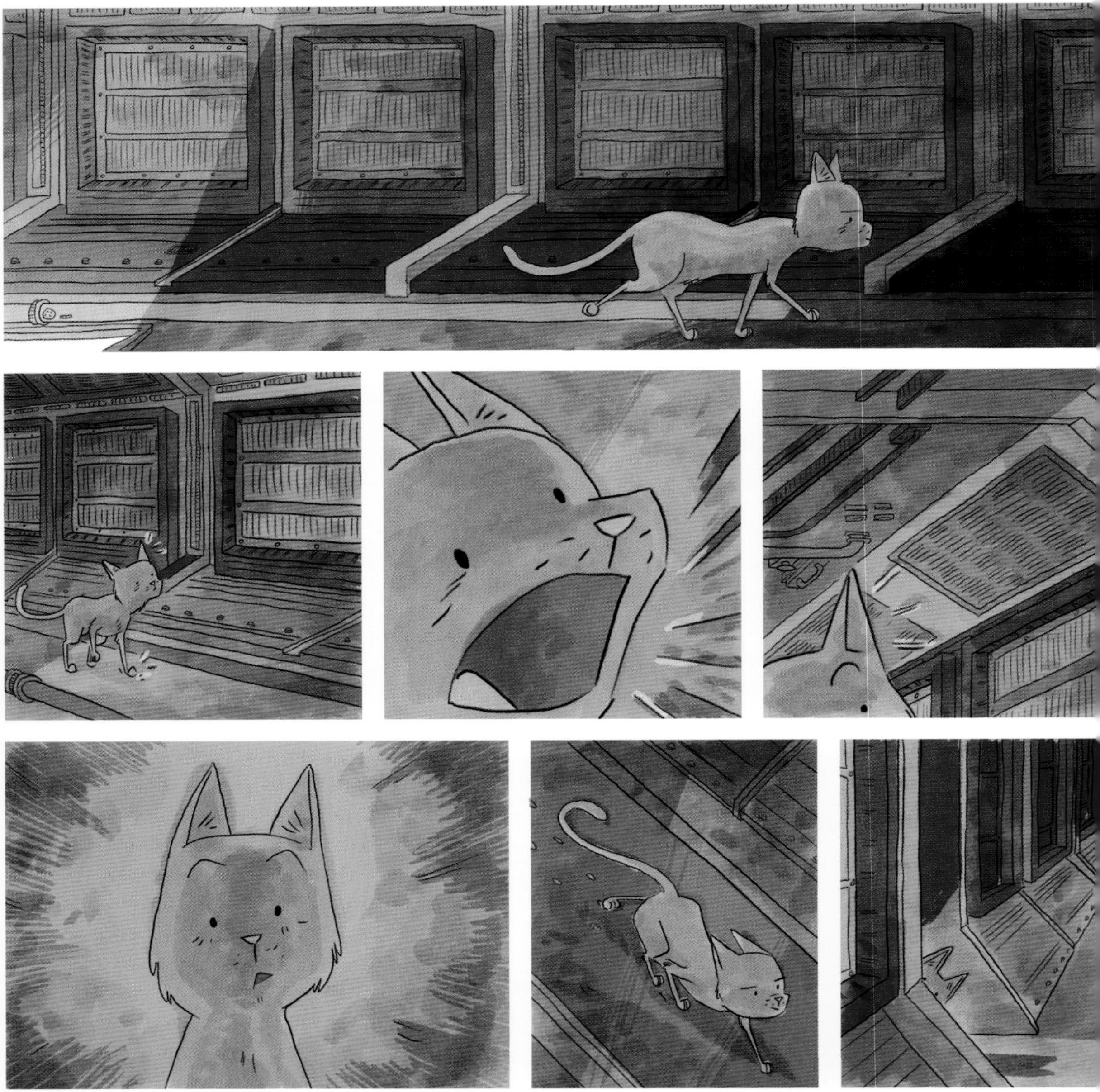

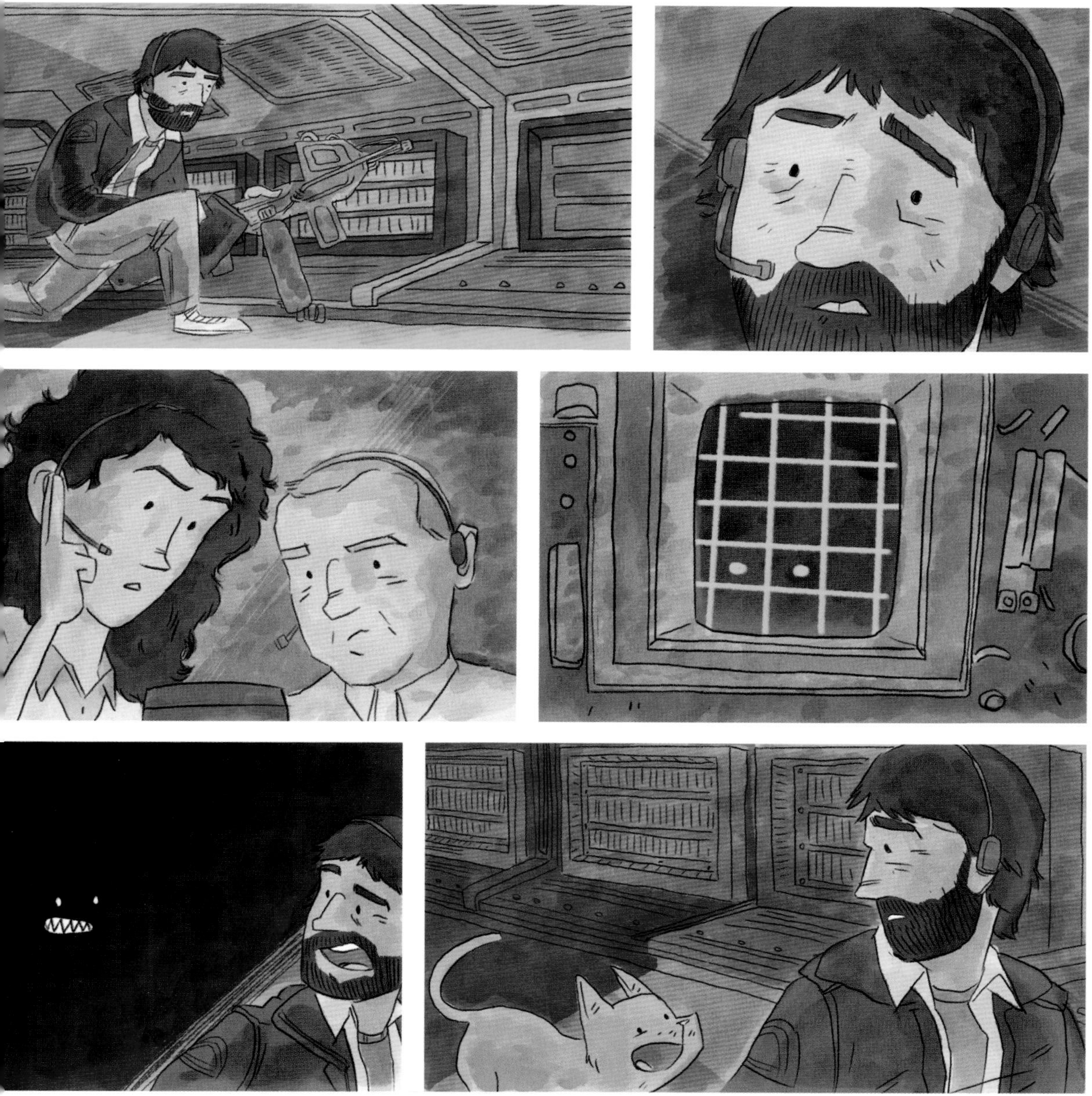

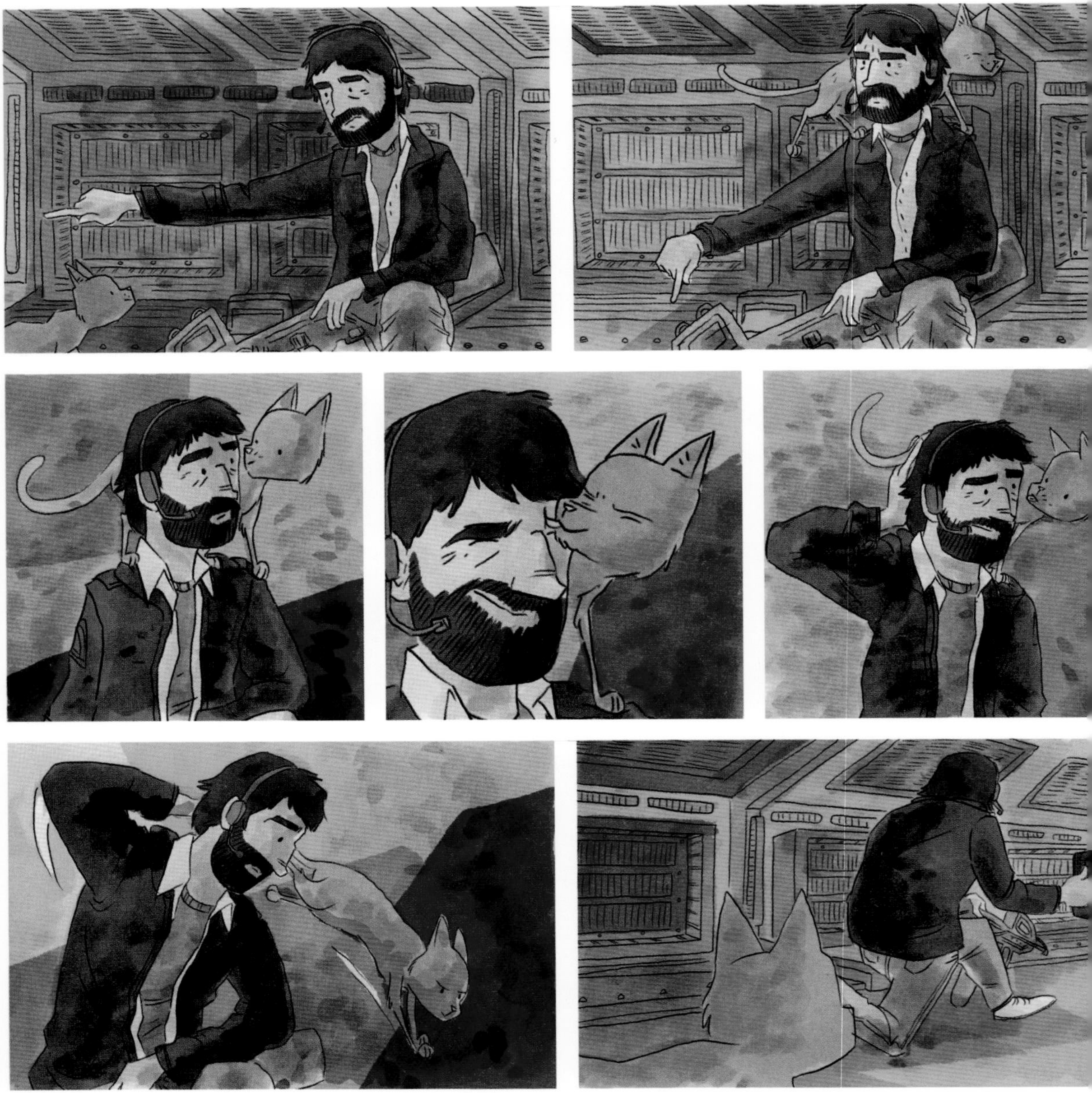

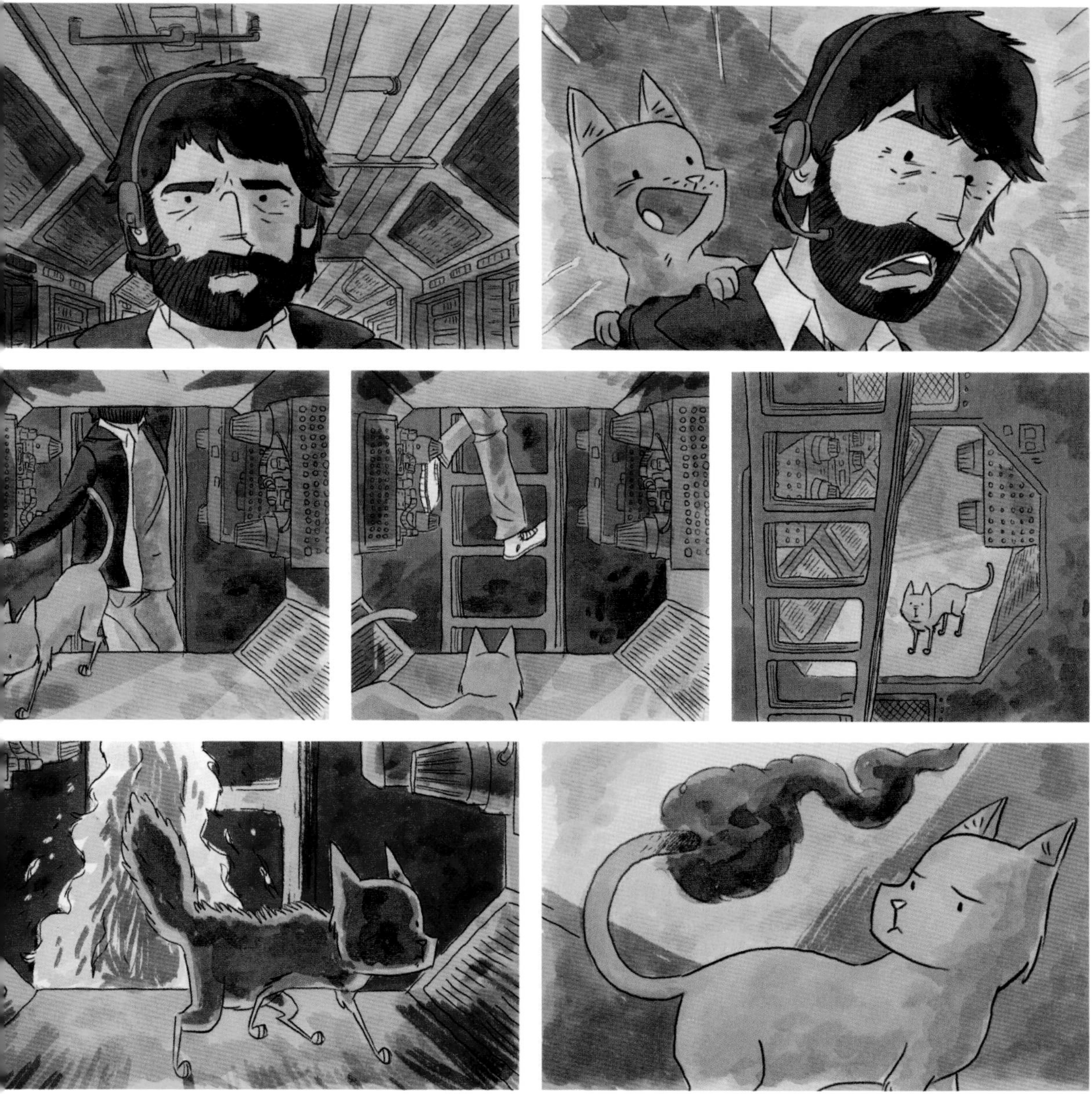

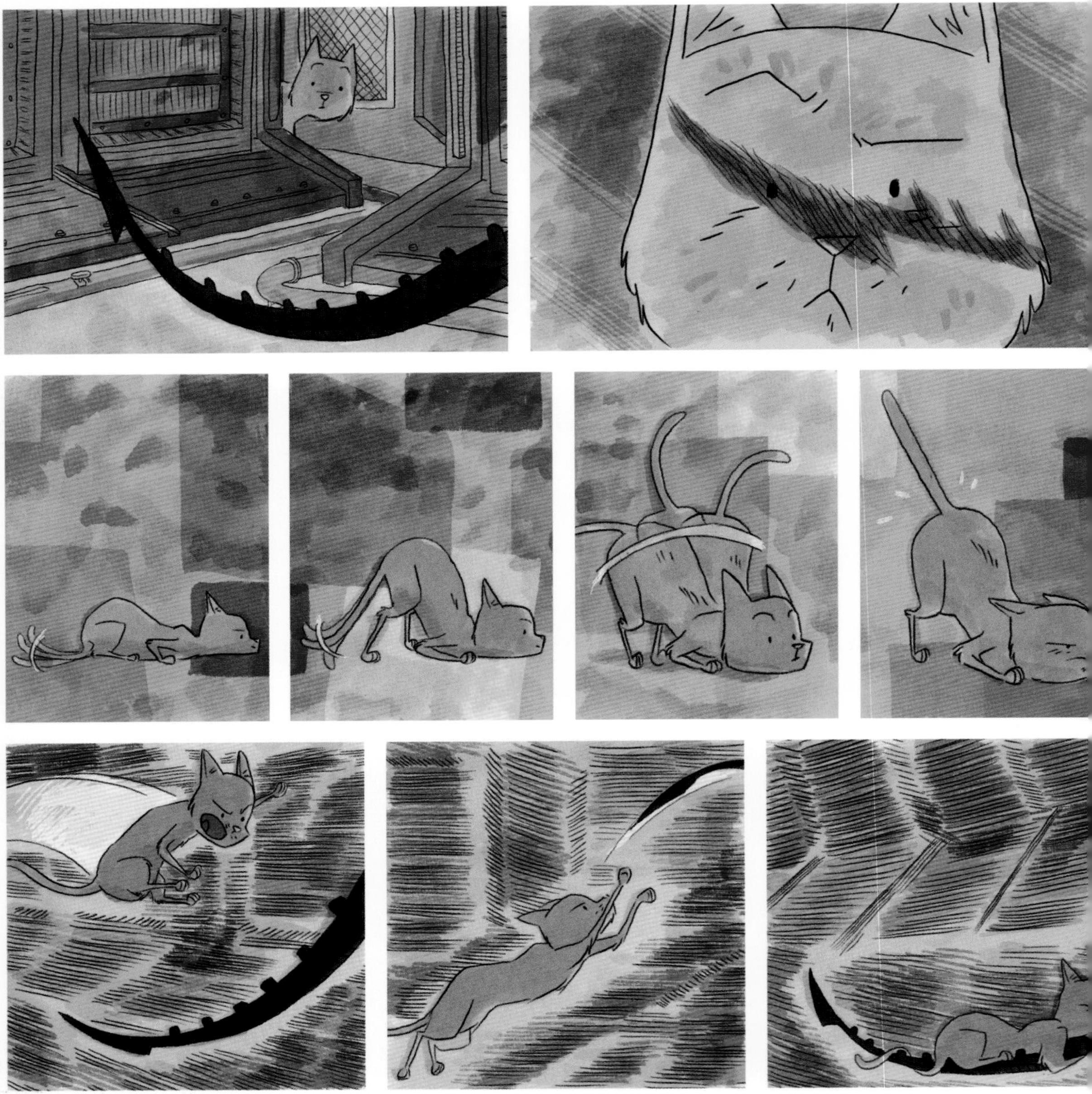

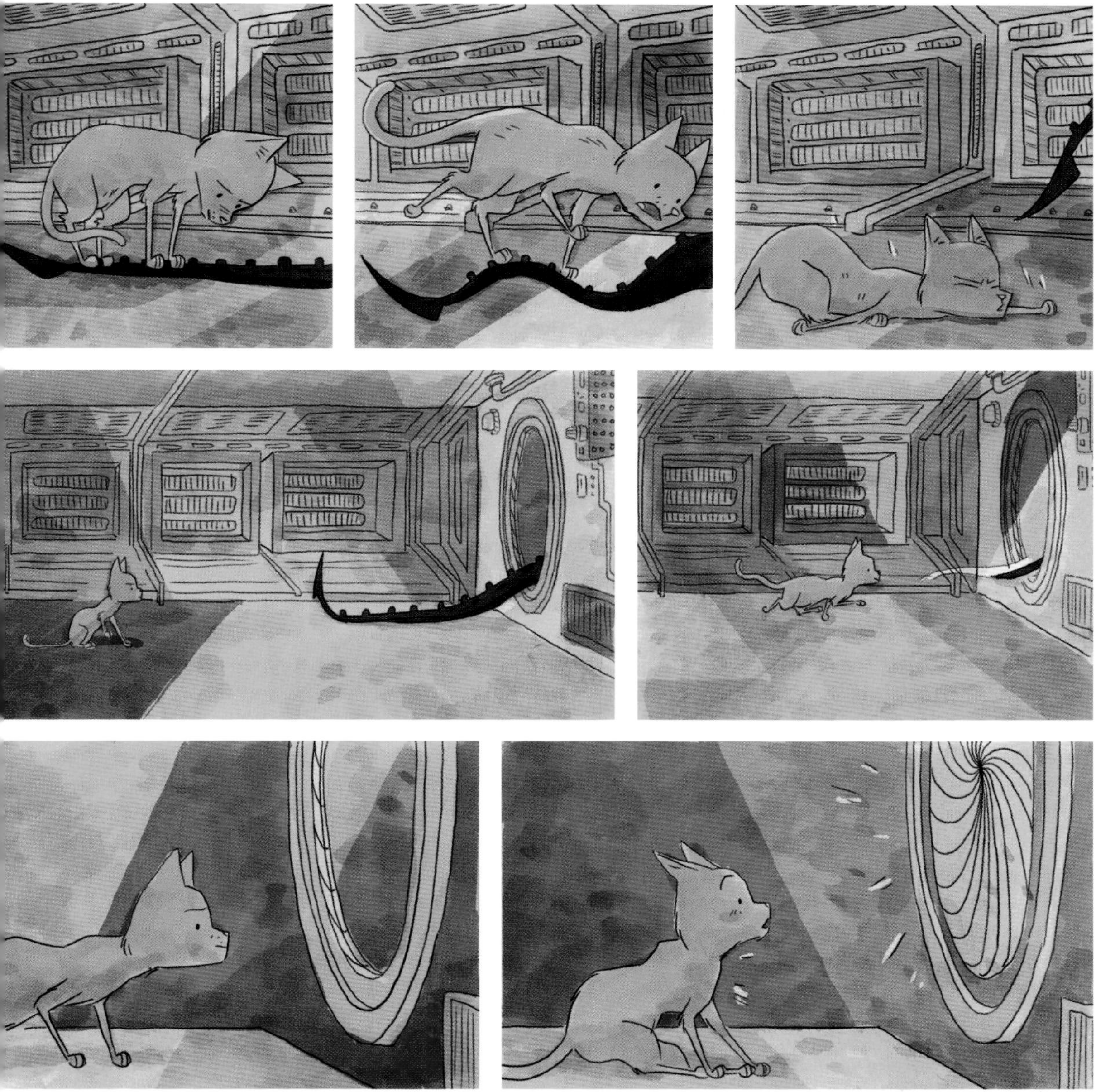

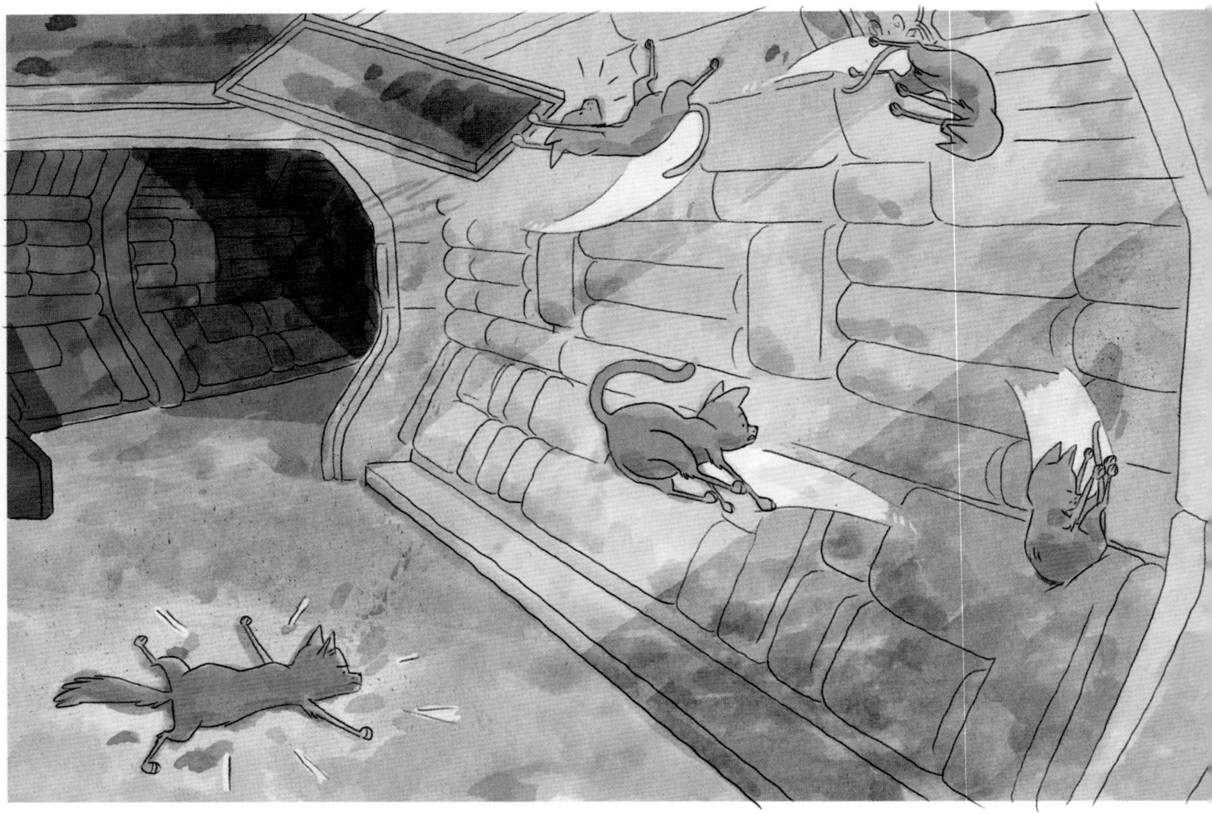
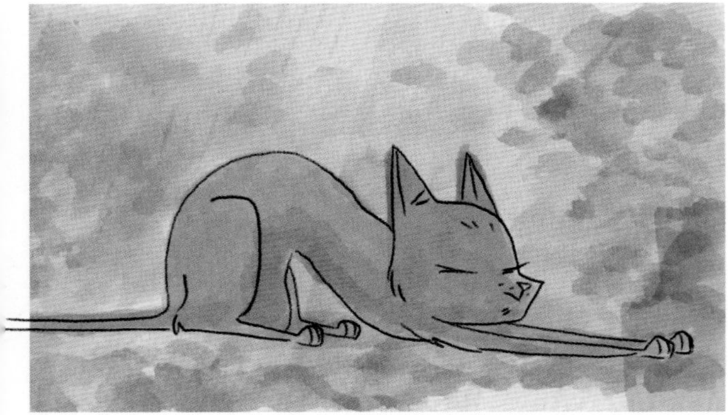
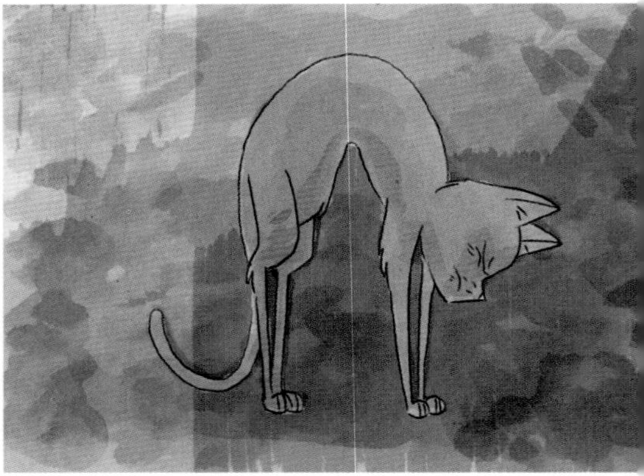

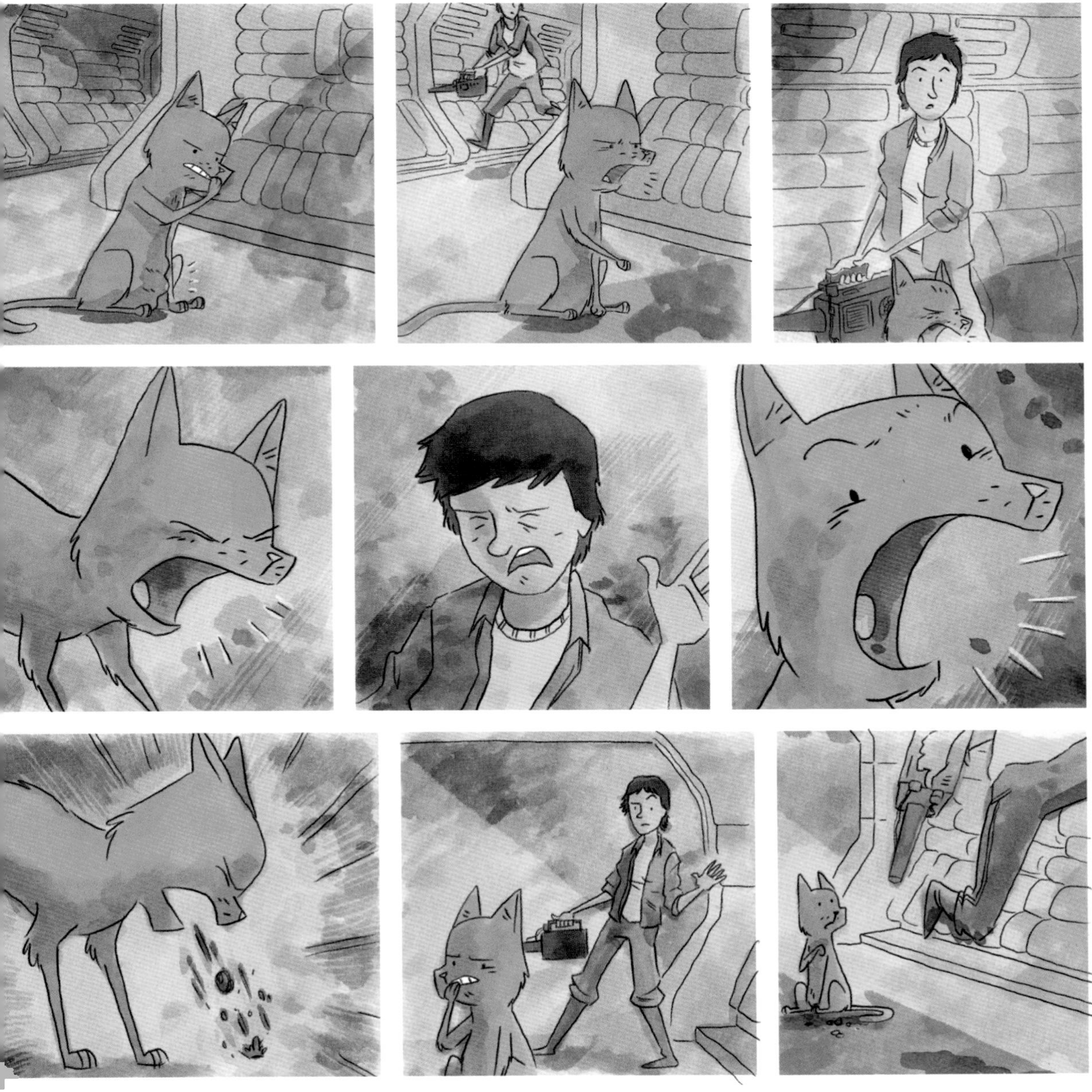

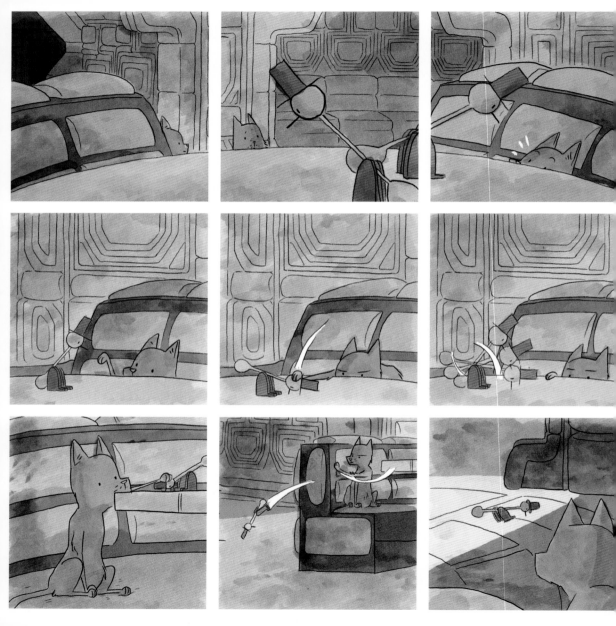

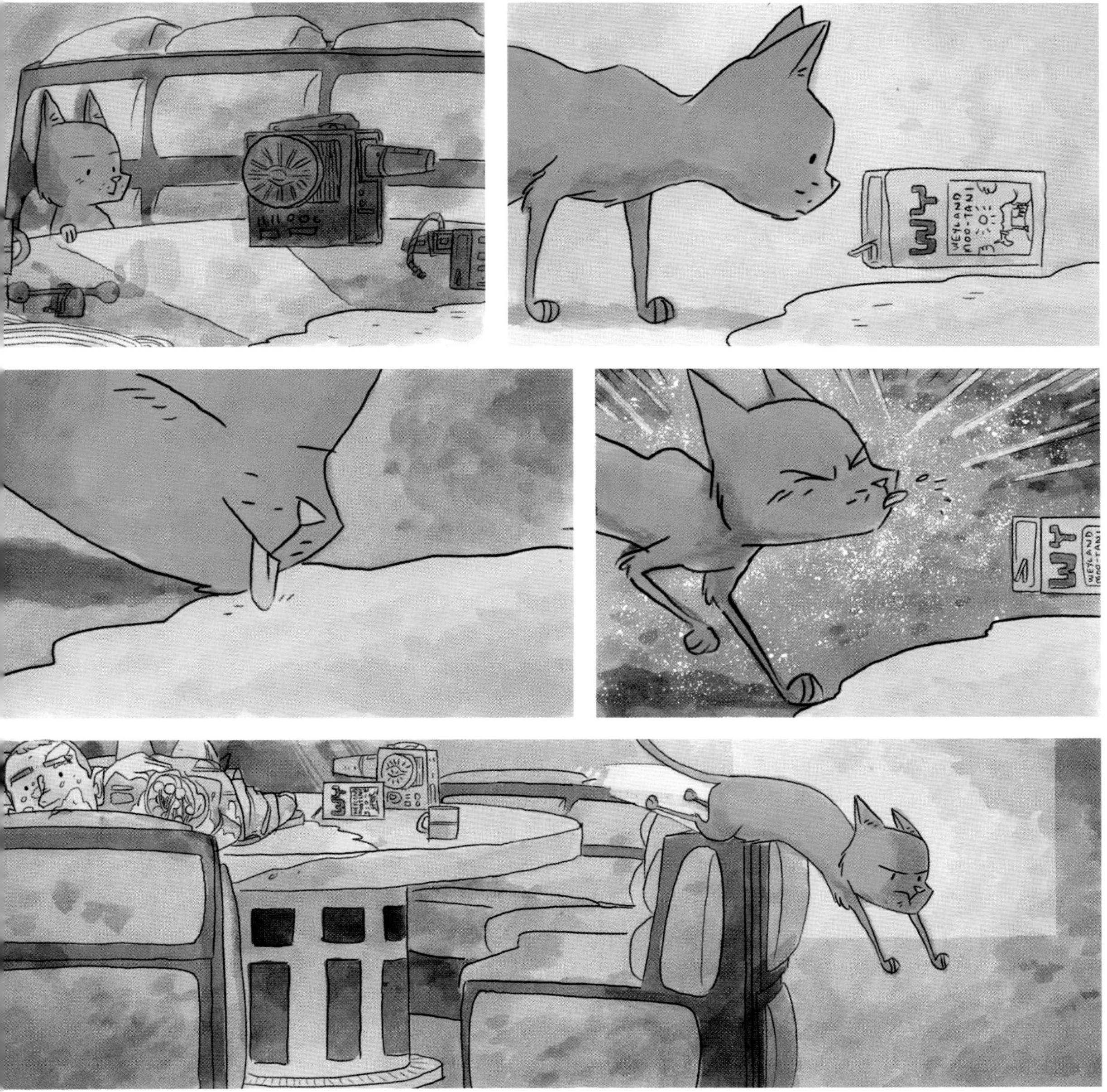
WEYLAND
MOO-TANI

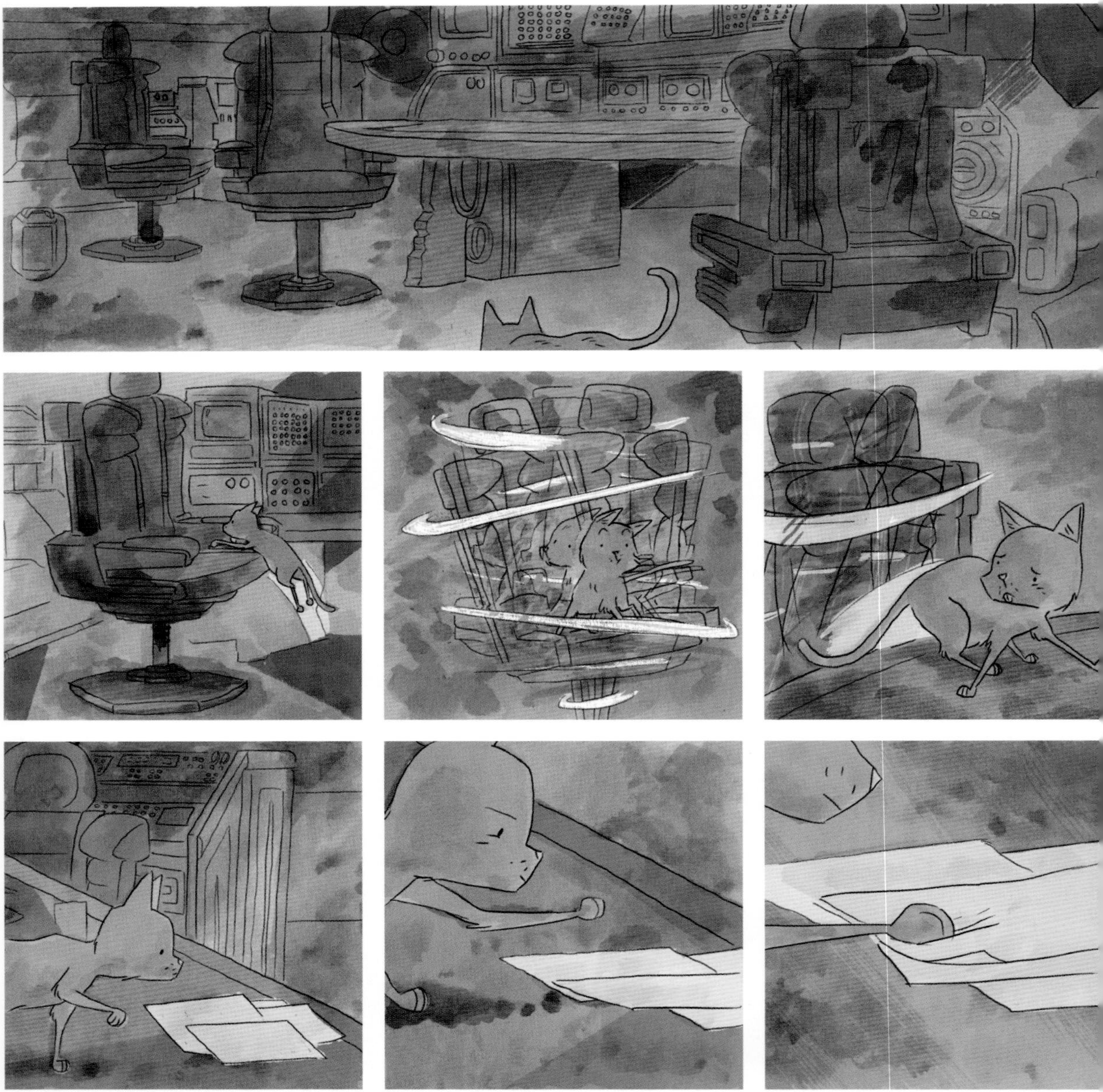

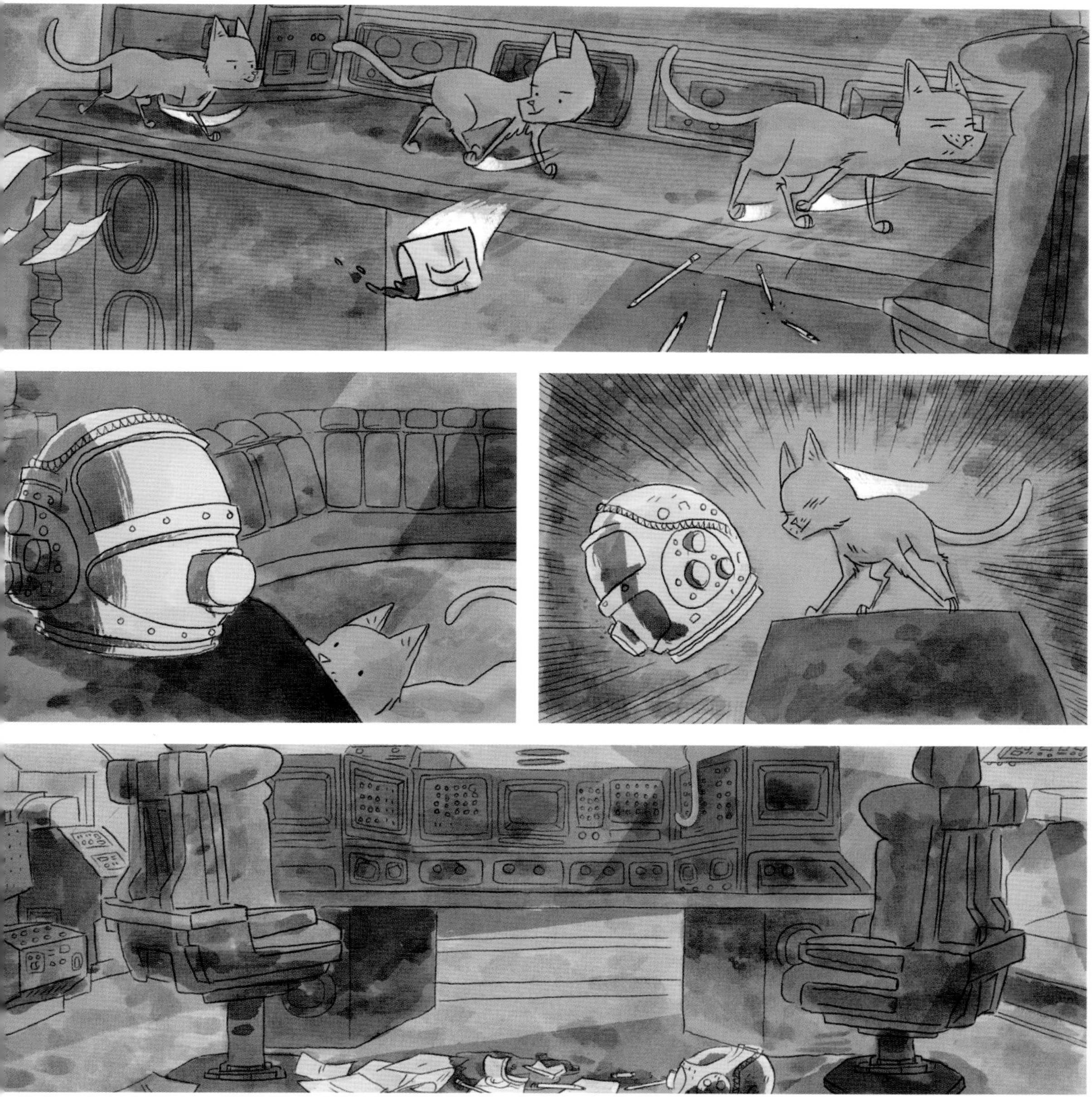

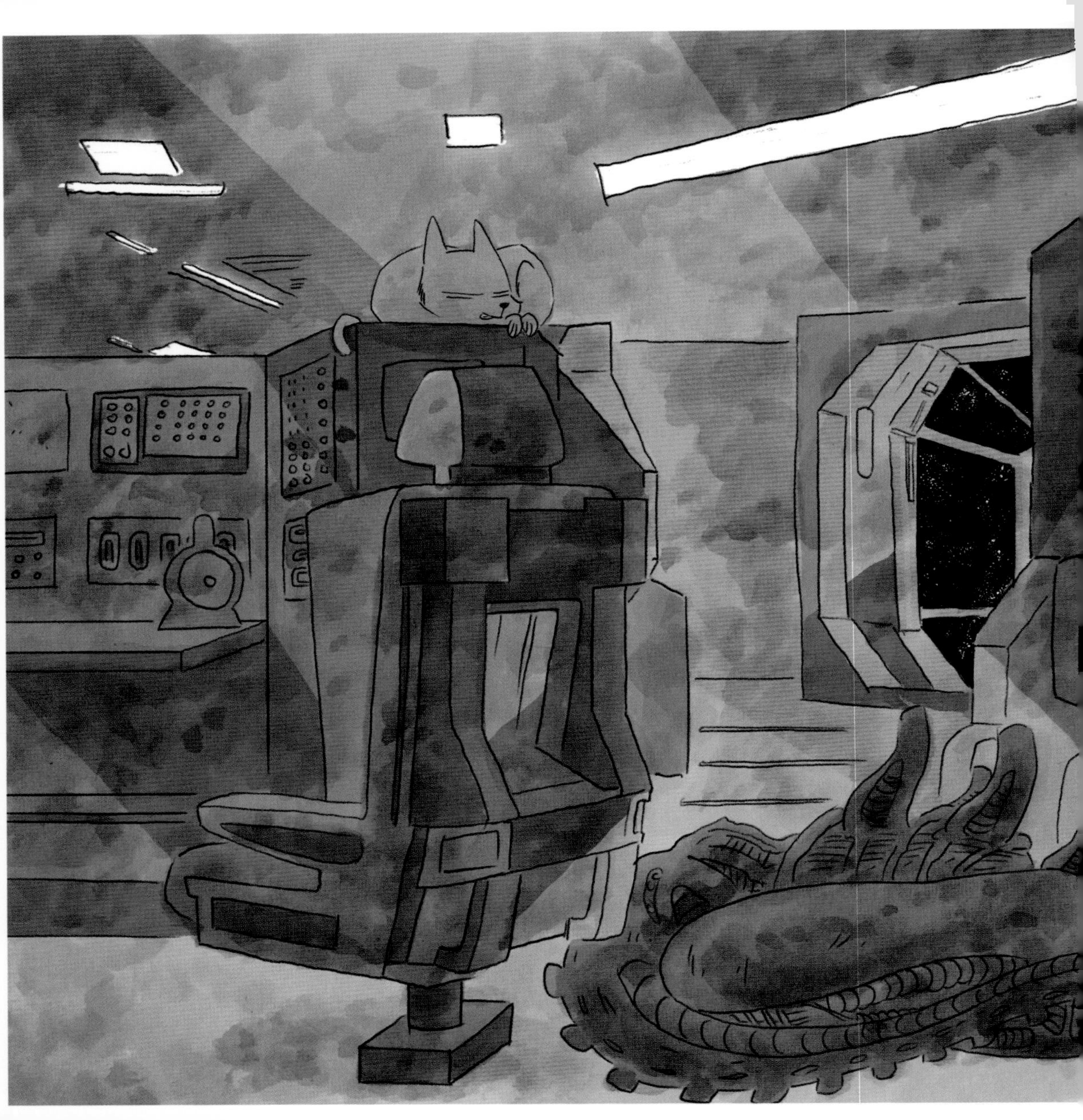

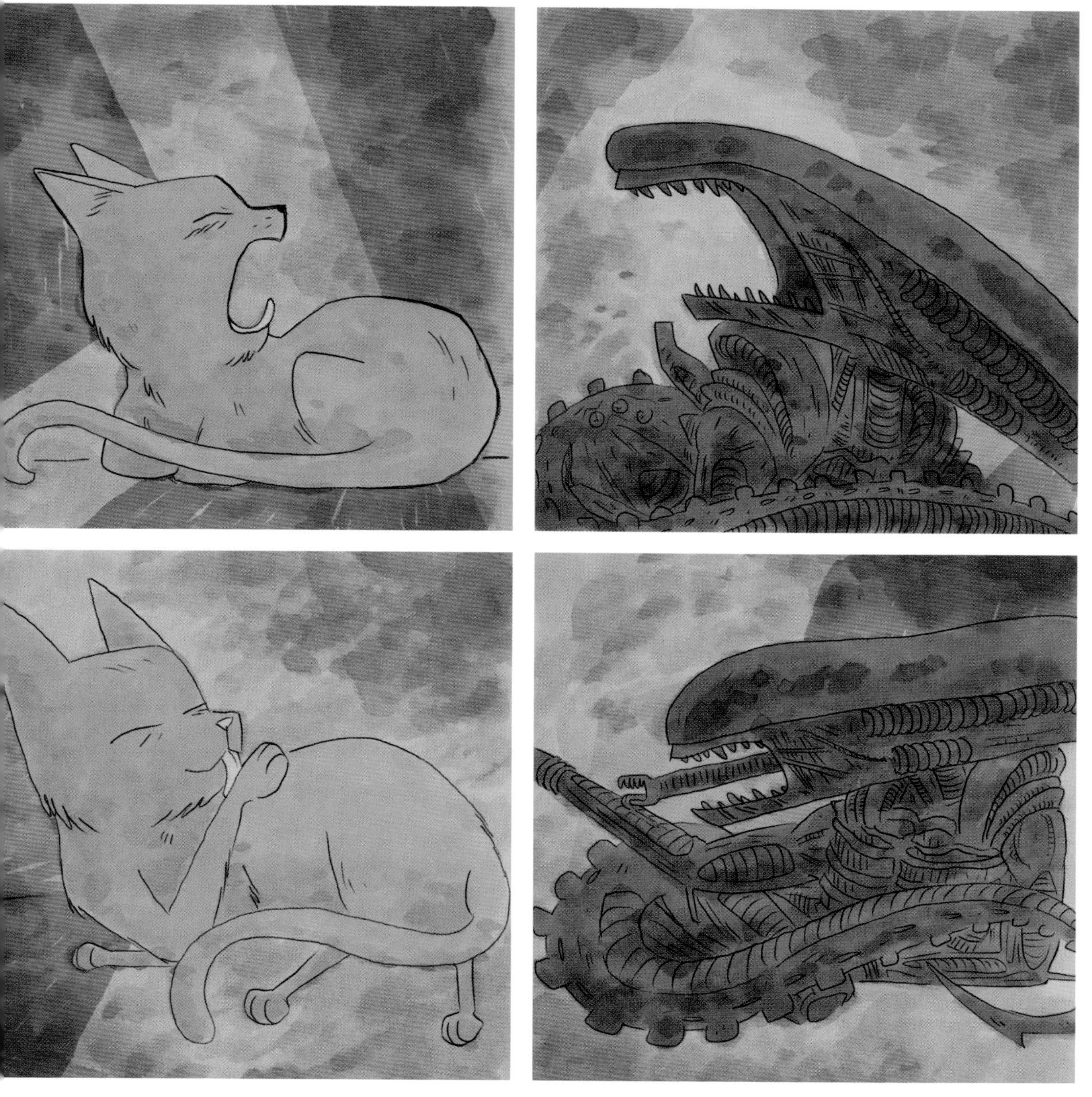

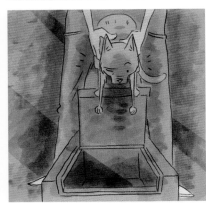
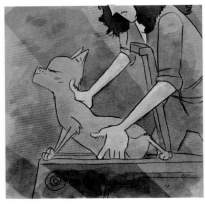

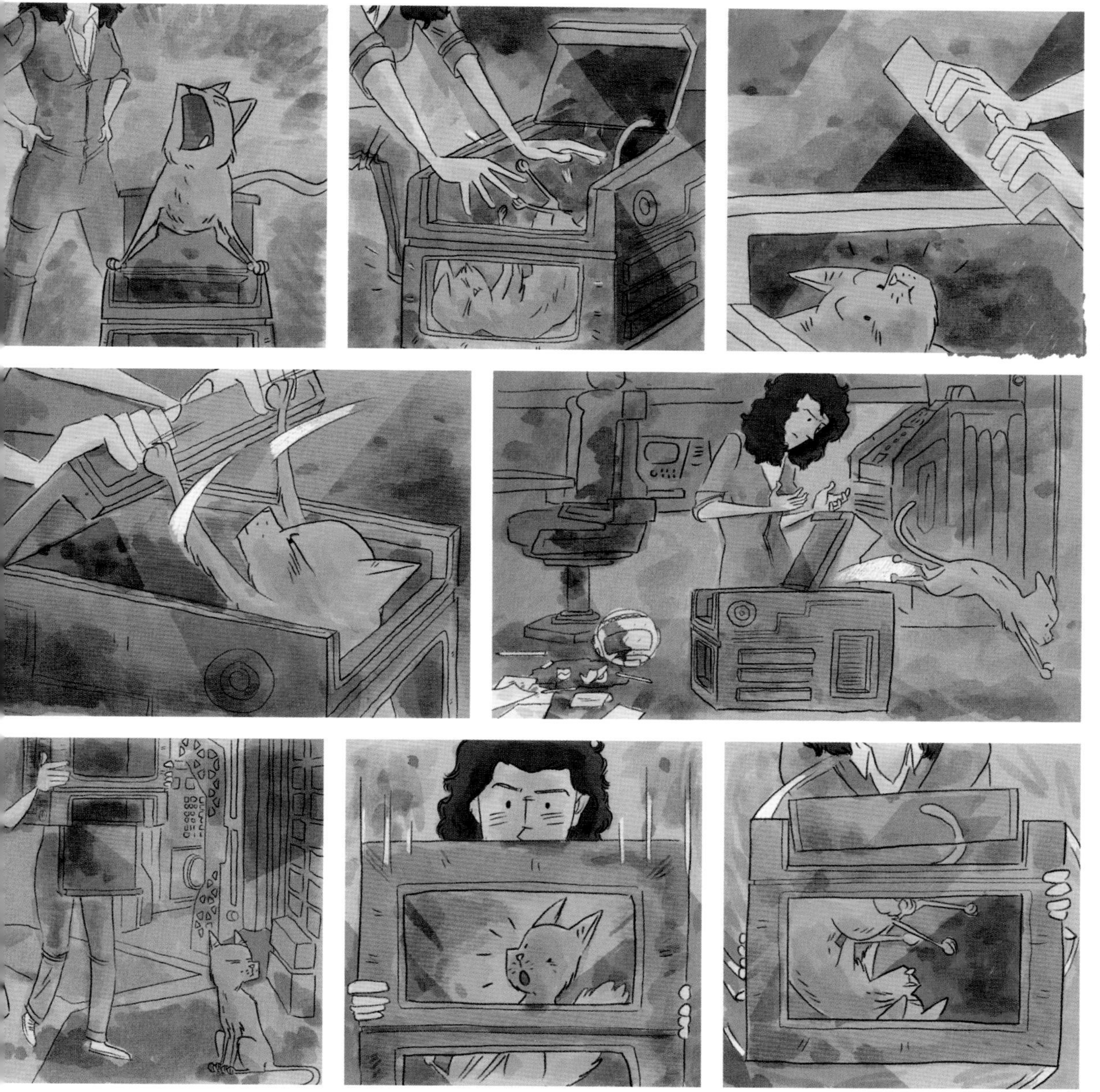

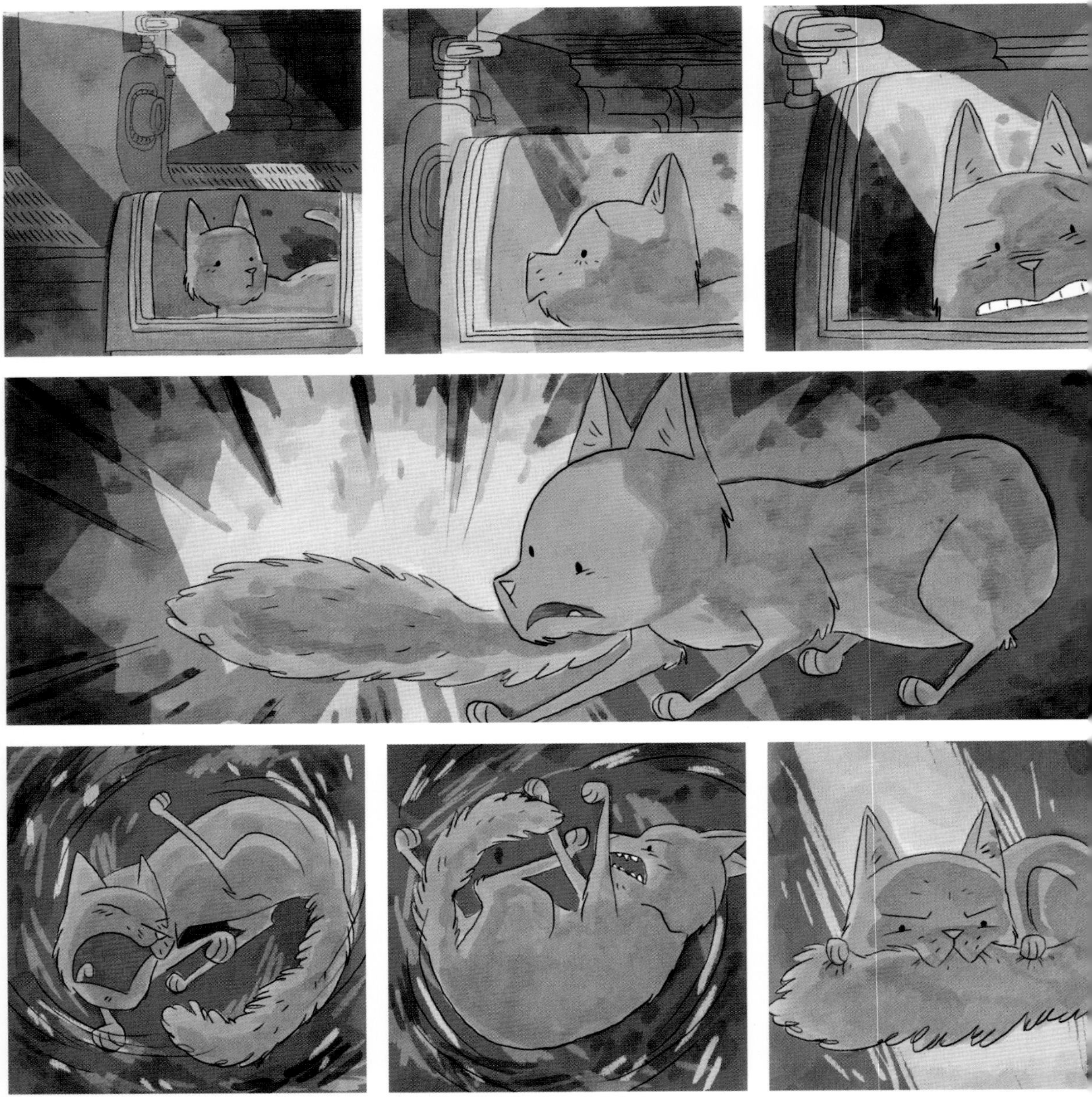

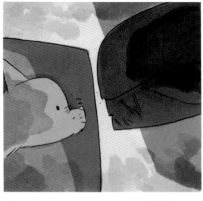

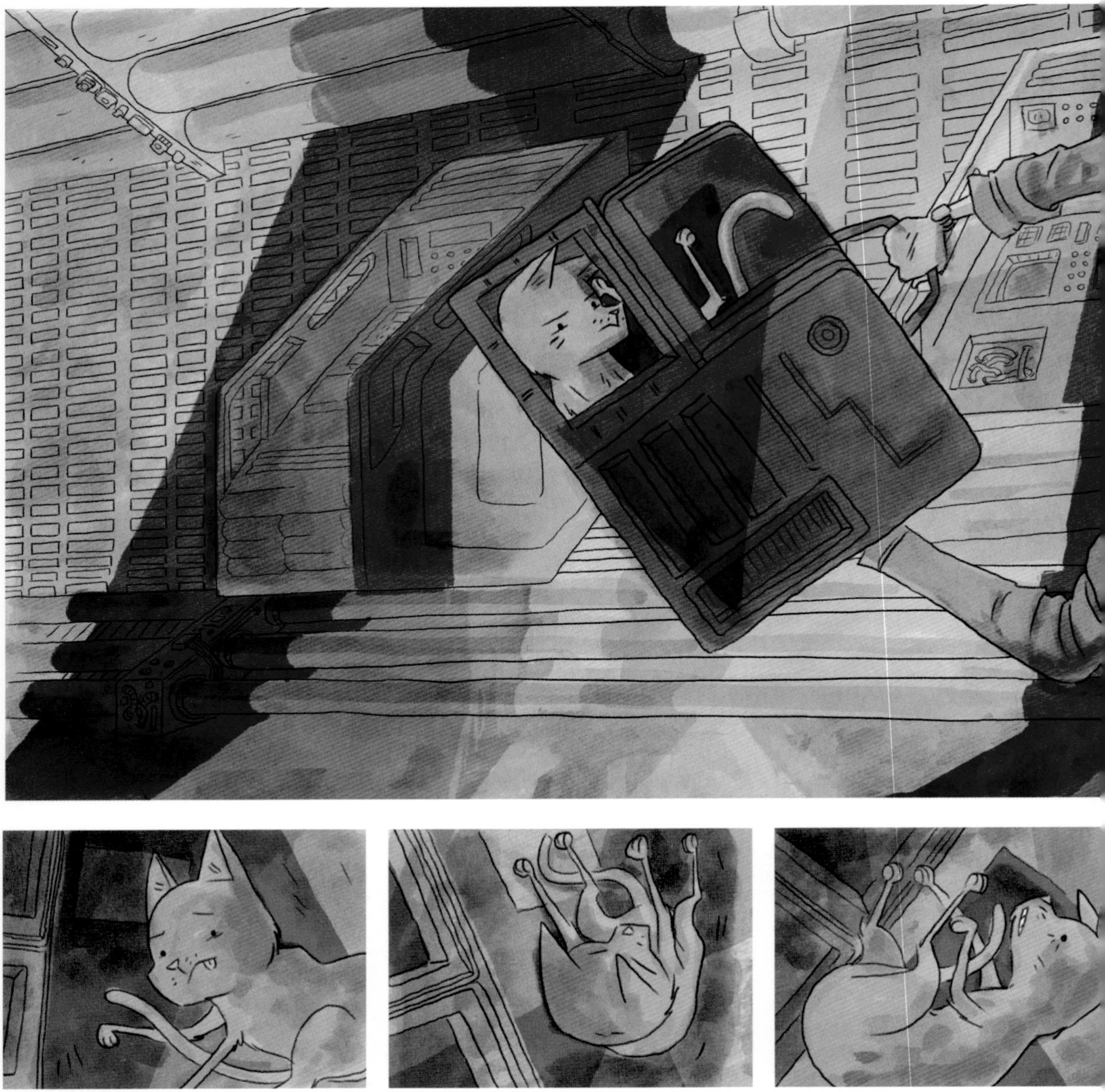

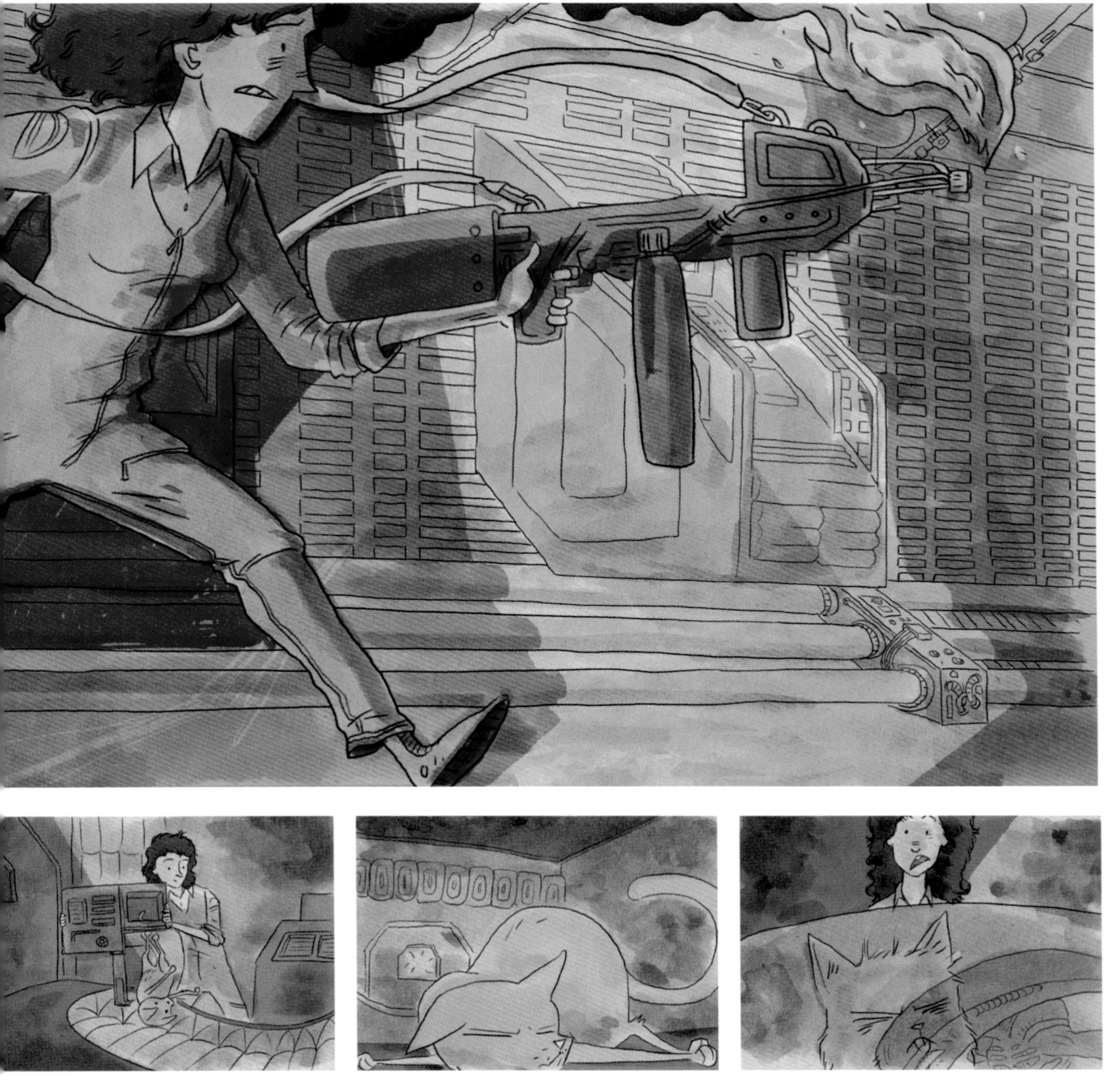

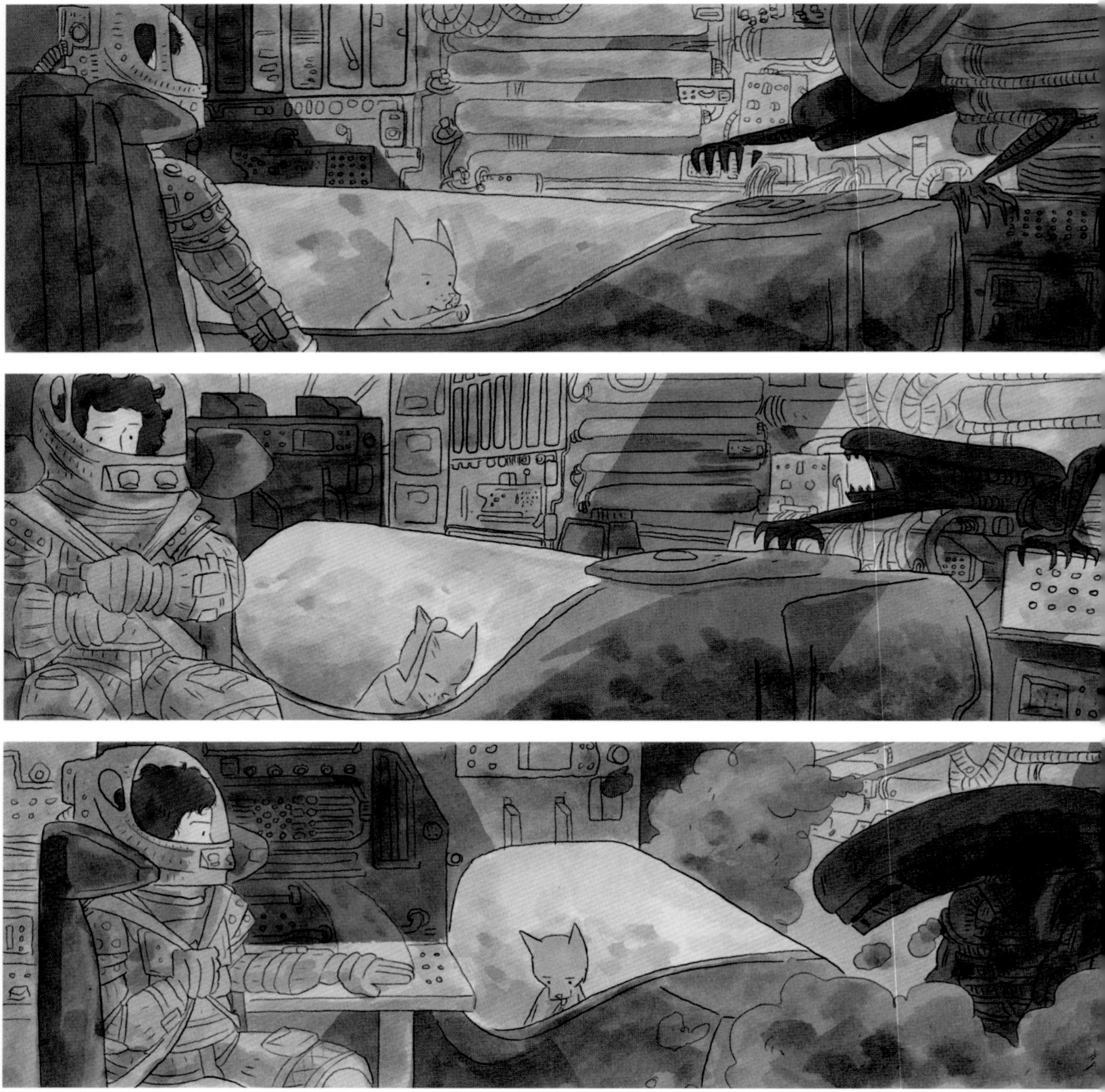

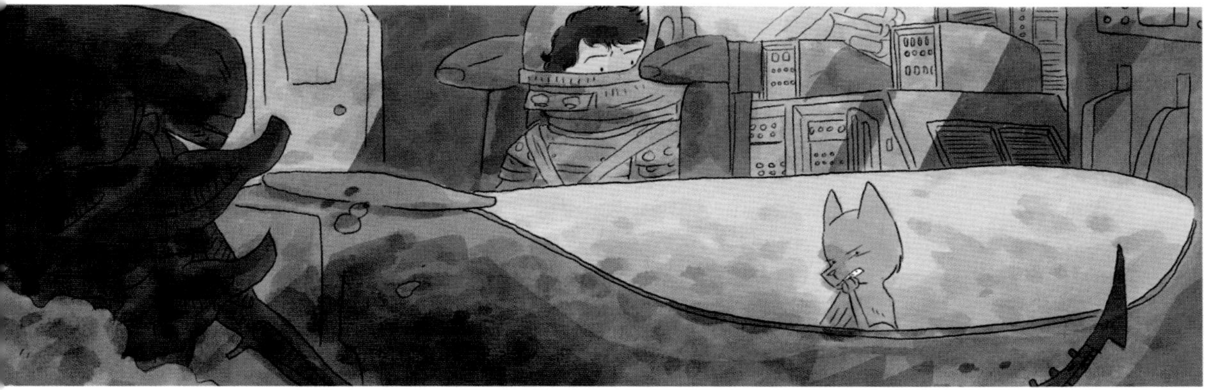
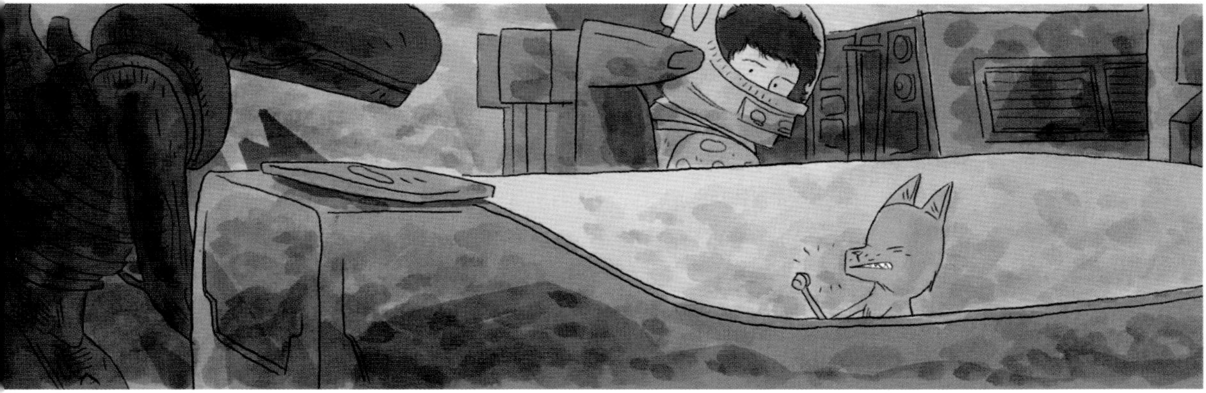
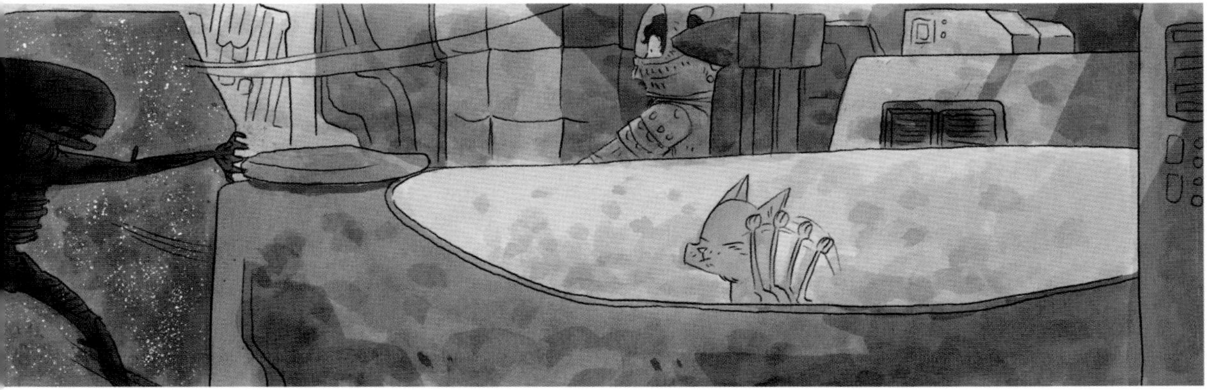

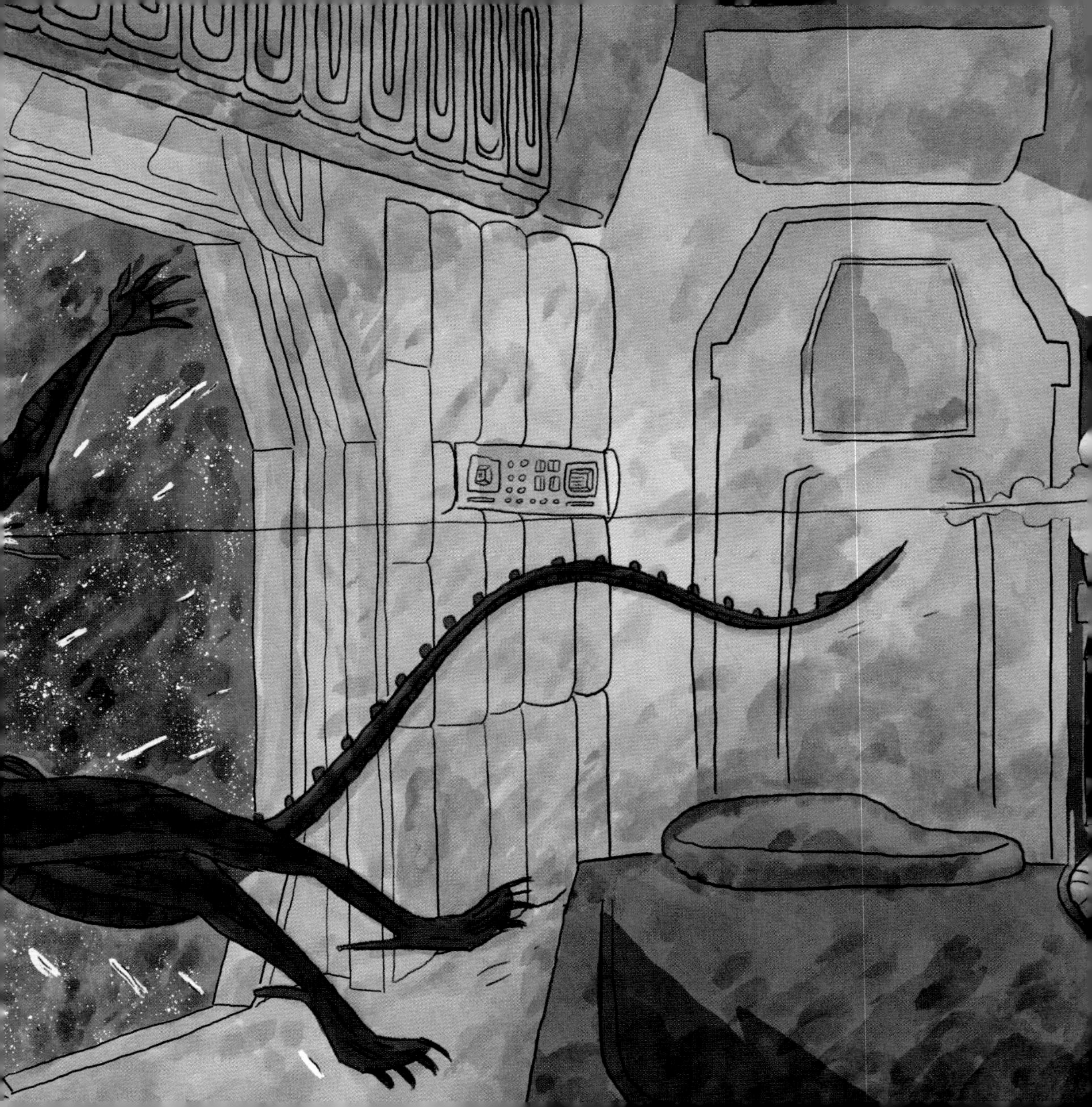

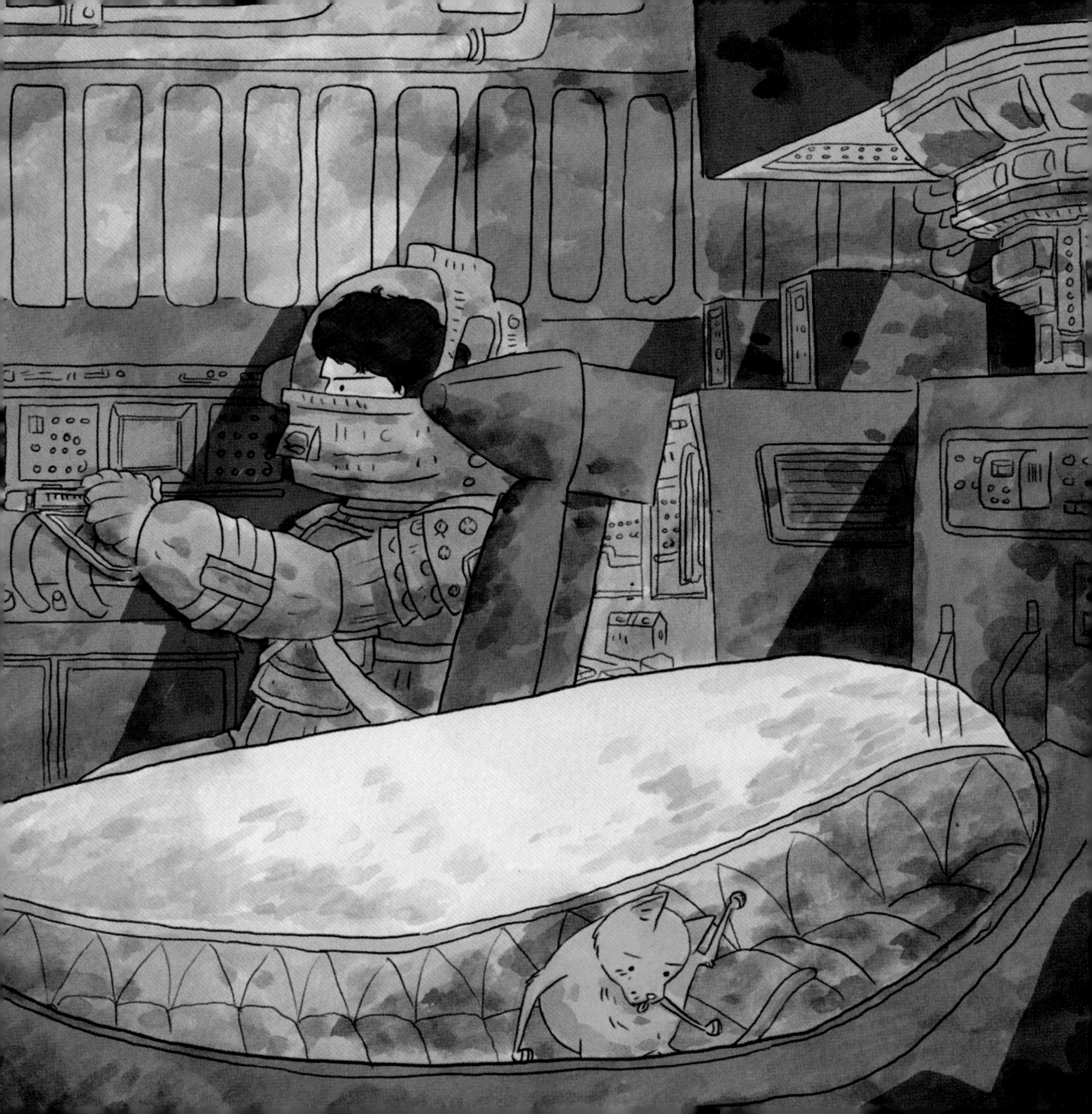

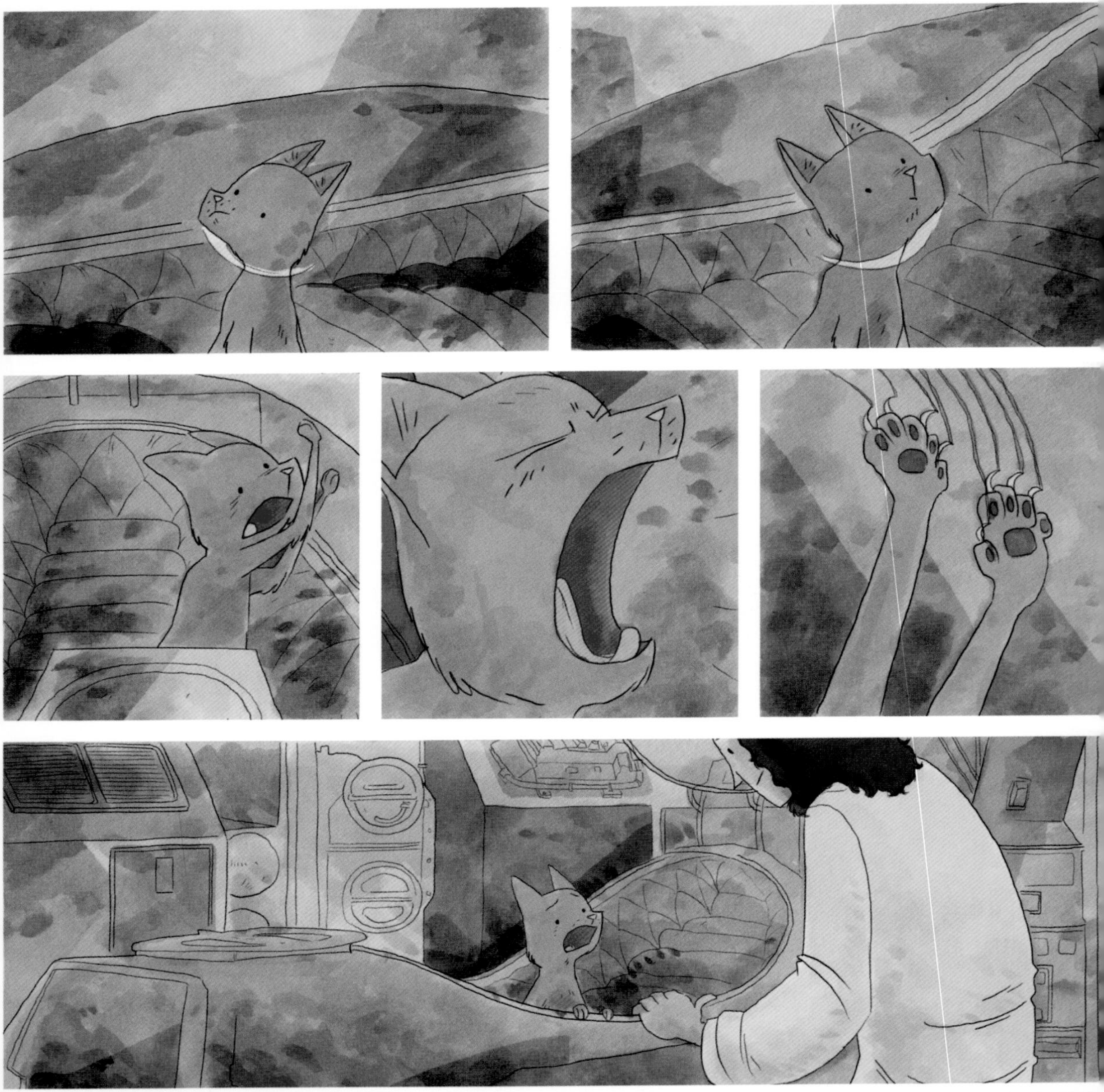

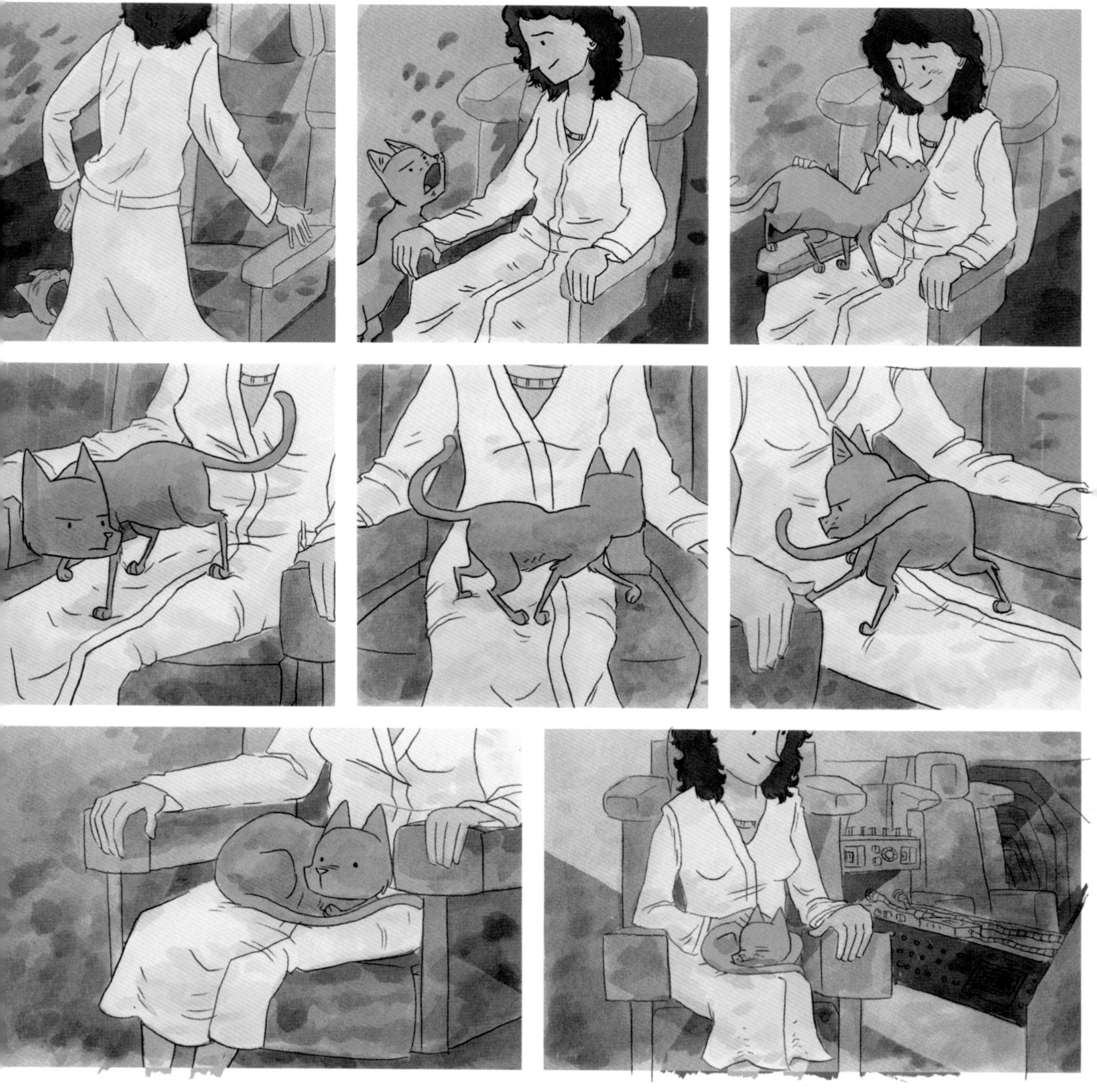

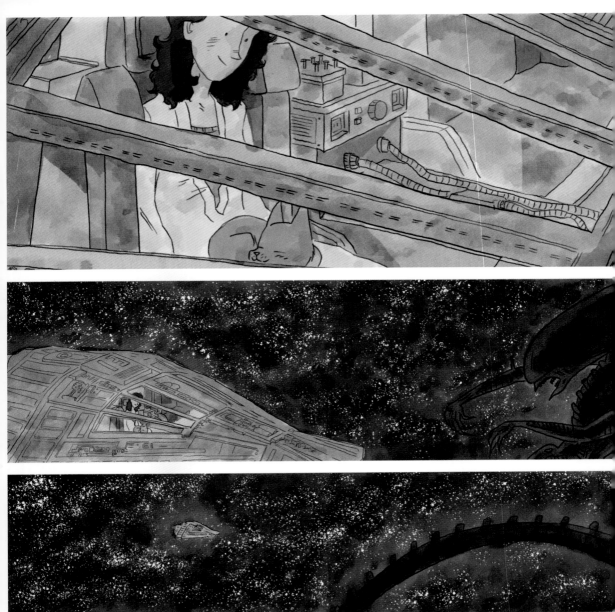

ACKNOWLEDGEMENTS

Many thanks to my family, friends, and supporters, especially Charlie Wilson and Simon Ward at Titan Books; Charlie Olsen at Inkwell; Neil Egan and Rebecca Hunt at Chronicle; Mum, Dad, Catherine, and Emer; and extra special thanks to Declan Hughes, Aidan Lucey, Emily Brennan, and Caesar.

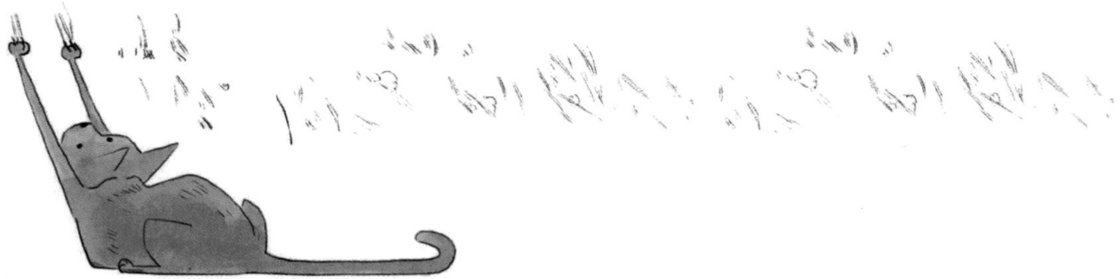